TO BE ONE OF US

SUNY Series, Philosophy of Education
Philip L. Smith, Editor

TO BE ONE OF US

Cultural Conflict, Creative Democracy, and Education

Nancy Warehime

Foreword by Robert McAfee Brown

State University of New York Press

Published by
State University of New York Press, Albany

For information, address State University of New York
Press, State University Plaza, Albany, N. Y. 12246

Production by Diane Ganeles
Marketing by Theresa A. Swierzowski

Library of Congress Cataloging-in-Publication Data

Warehime, Nancy, 1946-
    To be one of us : cultural conflict, creative democracy, and
education / Nancy Warehime.
        p. cm. — (SUNY series, philosophy of education)
    Includes bibliographical references (p.) and index.
    ISBN 0-7914-1321-7 (alk. paper). — ISBN 0-7914-1322-5 (pbk.
: alk. paper)
    1. Education, Higher—United States—Philosophy. 2. Educa-
tion, Higher—Social aspects—United States. 3. Education,
Humanistic—United States. 4. United States—Intellectual
life—20th century. I. Title. II. Series. III. Series: SUNY series
in philosophy of education.
LA227.4.W37 1993
378.73—dc20   92-3098
                                                                  CIP

10 9 8 7 6 5 4 3 2 1

For Ethan and Shane
and their parents
and
for Paul

Society will be moral to the extent that we see it in constant need of challenge, renewal, reconstruction. . . . A moral society will be perpetually unfinished.

—Robert McAfee Brown

Contents

Foreword:
"Here Be Dragons"

Ancient cartographers, after they had delimited the boundaries of the known world, would leave the remaining areas marked either "Unknown" (*Terra Incognita*) or identified with the legend "Here Be Dragons." To some, that was a warning to stay away; to others an invitation to explore.

Nancy Warehime has chosen to explore, and has provided a map for contemporary explorers who wish to examine with her the terrain of higher education, see what relationship it bears to the world around it, and what fresh contributions it might make.

That there are still dragons on the scene is not to be denied, but nowadays they are found within the territory of the "known" (*terra cognita*) rather than clinging precariously to the edges. Some dragons assume the posture of educational saviors and suggest that the *real* dragons are all masquerading as their critics. Others believe that what counts right now is to issue stiff challenges to everybody, and for them the dragons are those with relatively self-assured points of view. (The quality of "dragon-ness," as we learned when we graduated from the nursery, is chiefly in the eye of the beholder.)

The dragon image will have served its purpose if it secures the notion that the issues under exploration in this book are serious matters, with important (even life-and-death) consequences, and that the contestants in the drama are not just playing games, but are putting a great deal on the line—everything (according to who is talking) from their own intellectual acuity to the fate of Western Civilization, plus a good deal in between.

Anyone who ventures to discuss the moral implications of a given subject matter such as education, is asking for trouble. Much safer, the "wise" will tell us, to keep distanced from the subject matter, to be reportorial rather than involved, or to let others work on the "implications." Fortunately for her readers, Dr. Warehime rejects such advice. She is not only a map-maker but a participant in what is happening on the terrain she has pictured for us. Not to put too fine a point on it, *she takes sides*. She sees "education as an agent of moral development and the formation of the good society," an approach by no means universally accepted or even respected in some quarters. Out of a jumble of competing moral claims—in a world where those who claim not to be raising moral claims should be most suspect—she arrives at a position of her own, and by the integrity of her investigation is urging her readers to do the same. So while these pages are, formally, an "academic exercise," they are more than an exclusively academic exercise. They are (if one can say it without being misunderstood) an exercise of the spirit, of the whole person.

There is no need to summarize the themes here. They lie directly before us on the succeeding pages, in which three important and very different views of the educational enterprise are accurately expounded, clearly differentiated, and capably criticized. I had no idea when I began how intrigued I would become with the discussion, and how eagerly I would await not only the next section listed in the Contents, but also the author's own assessments along the way. I soon found that I trusted her fairness, her convictions, her values, and her invitation to be part of the exchange myself.

I will, however, mention one further characteristic of the text before us. This is the wide reach of the author's reading and concerns. The intramural examination of Allan Bloom, Richard Rorty, and Cornel West is graced by insights and individuals far removed from that immediate context, and enlivening and enriching the whole. I refer, to give only a few examples, to such things as the telling use of Martin Luther King's "Letter from a Birmingham Jail," at the very outset; the ongoing conversation with Albert Camus; the elucidation of the Hebrew prophetic tradition as well as the rational tradition of the Greeks; the reclaiming of John Dewey as partner to the discussion; the introduction of critiques by women of the calibre of Nancy Fraser; the sensitive discussion of the possibility (or impossibility) of "the noble lie;" the use of an Asian thinker like Kosuke Koyama to broaden the horizon; the willingness to speak some good words for compassion; the introduction of Gramsci, a Marxist who must still be taken seriously even as Marxism is going through troubled times; the recognition that "nonmetaphysical" thought structures are rife with metaphysical underpinnings; the ongoing insistence that the political consequences (or presuppositions) of a theory of education are desperately important to everyone.

Let us, with some reticence, allow the dragons back on stage. For Dr. Warehime's text has helped me to identify more clearly than I have done before, a few that I would like some latter-day St. George to dispatch for me. (1) Chief among them is the dragon of *elitism*—not only the claim that intellectuals alone count, but that among the intellectuals Asians don't count, women don't count, the poor don't count. (2a) Also high on the list is the dragon of *disengagement*— the notion that the practice of "education" is a few privileged people exchanging views without any concern for the fate of the rest of the world, coupled with a studied disdain of "relevance" as a kind of intellectual pandering for the approval of the masses. (2b) Tied for second place is a characteristic both the above positions exemplify, a claim by the dragon of *objectivity*—the notion that I can really shed my skin, or my personal history, or my class orientation, and deal, without presuppositions and without rancor or self-interest, with matters that are of crucial importance to others. The notion that I do not bring all that baggage (and much more) to my intellectualizing, strikes me as serious self-delusion. (3) Finally, the dragon of *dogmatism*—a scaly monster of whom to be particularly aware. Dispelling this dragon does not mean shedding one's convictions. It does mean voicing one's convictions in such a way that one remains open to learning from others, from history, and from one's own experience, not to mention cultivating a healthy recognition of the deep insecurity that sometimes entices us to clothe ourselves in apparently invincible armor.

In girding ourselves to do battle with such dragons in the groves of *academe,* we should be particularly grateful to Dr. Warehime for rediscovering Paul Tillich's distinction between "the utopian spirit" and an "absolutized utopia." The "utopian spirit" is a drive and a yearning for a better society, with ever-new possibilities, whereas an "absolutized utopia" is a society that can no longer afford to be open, but must defend its "achievements" against all challenge, by use of force if necessary. As Dr. Tillich points out wisely: "It is the spirit of utopia that conquers utopia."

Dragons who hear that word will tremble.

ROBERT McAFEE BROWN

Acknowledgments

In its first life, this book was my doctoral dissertation at Iowa State University. In that setting, I was bolstered, both intellectually and morally, by two teachers and friends, Robert Hollinger and David Owen, who steadfastly believed in the significance of my work. Both of these men, by virtue of their shared moral temperament, were ideal midwives throughout the birthing process.

After I left Iowa State, the ideas contained in this book fermented for a year at Drury College in Springfield, Missouri, where my professional responsibilities were divided between the Department of Religion and Philosophy and the college chaplaincy. At Drury came the opportunity for praxis, for living out "creative democracy" with my colleagues and students. My year at Drury proved to be an existential touchstone against which to take stock of my intellectual and moral claims. While I hesitate to mention anyone by name—precisely because of the relational richness of the Drury community—I am particularly grateful to Dick and Jean Killough, Charles and Conni Ess, Judith Armstrong, and Ruth Bamberger, all of whom embody a politically fertile spirituality.

Others who have helped to bring my observations into their present form are Judy Jarboe, who carefully and cheerfully typed each variation from dissertation to book manuscript; and Lois Patton and Phil Smith, both of whom offered warm—and timely—encouragement.

Finally, my companion, Paul Hollenbach, has been a gracious, stimulating, and steadfast presence through the changing seasons and long miles of this book's evolution. For both "loaves and hyacinths," I am in his debt.

Excerpts from *The Closing of the American Mind,* copyright © 1987 by Allan Bloom, reprinted by permission of Simon and Schuster, Inc.

Excerpts from "Solidarity or Singularity? Richard Rorty Between Romanticism & Techocracy" by Nancy Fraser. In *Praxis International* 8 (October 1988). Reprinted by permission of Blackwell Publishers.

Excerpts from *Criticism and Social Change* copyright © 1983 by Frank Lentricchia, reprinted by permission of University of Chicago Press.

Excerpts from *Mount Fuji and Mount Sinai* copyright © 1984 by Kosuke Koyama, reprinted by permission of SCM Press Ltd, and of Orbis Books (USA Publication © 1985).

Excerpts from *Contingency, irony and solidarity,* copyright © 1989 by Richard Rorty, reprinted by permission of Cambridge University Press.

Excerpts from "Hermeneutics, General Studies and Teaching" by Richard Rorty. Copyright © 1982 by Synergos Seminars. Reprinted by permission of the editor, Vernon Gras.

Other acknowledgments appear on pages containing copyrighted material. My thanks to all those who granted permission for reprinting.

Preface

If the ruling and the oppressed elements in a population, if those who wish to maintain the status quo and those concerned to make changes, had, when they became articulate, the same philosophy, one might well be skeptical of its intellectual integrity.

The task of democracy is forever that of creation of a freer and more humane experience in which all share and to which all contribute.

—John Dewey

In April of 1963, Martin Luther King, Jr. was among those arrested in Birmingham, Alabama, for taking part in mass protests against segregation of public facilities in that city. While imprisoned, King wrote his famous "Letter from Birmingham Jail," in which he responded to criticisms leveled against his "direct action" by white church leaders. For King, the moral imperatives of Christian tradition were clear in relation to the evils of institutionalized racism. But many others who embraced the same tradition perceived different imperatives. Some of this latter group were sympathetic with King but urged him to be patient, to break no laws, to do nothing "extreme" which might precipitate violence. These individuals saddened King, but they did not baffle him. He admonished them to abandon the "anesthetizing security of stained-glass windows," to rediscover the "creative extremism" of their own tradition, and to keep faith with it by coming "to the aid of justice." Others who claimed loyalty to the Christian tradition were more of a mystery to King. These persons were "outright opponents" of the freedom movement; their attitudes and behaviors were so at odds with King's understanding of Christianity that he was driven to ask, "Who is their God?"

King's letter from prison is a passionate appeal to the church to keep faith with its gospel by joining the struggle "to set at liberty those who are oppressed" (Luke 4:18). Put another way, King challenges the institution which claims to be the embodiment of traditional moral authority in the name of traditional moral authority itself. Importantly, he supports his moral challenge by situating Christian tradition in social/historical context, not by attempting to establish metaphysical proofs. He does not claim to have discovered or created moral truth. Rather, he appeals to a history, a tradition, which is as readily available to his listeners as it is to him.* But King's question "Who is their God?" illustrates the vast differences which exist between his moral sensibilities and the sensibilities of those Christians who oppose the freedom movement. These differences, in turn, indicate that the content of Christian tradition is itself a matter of contention. The complexities of interpretation in relation to moral authority thus become painfully apparent.

King's moral challenge to the institutionalized church epitomizes the social strife of the 1960s. In that tumultuous decade virtually every cultural institution—both religious and secular—which claimed to embody and defend the values of Western democracy was challenged *on moral grounds*. Thus, as opposed to what Allan Bloom and others of his persuasion continue to argue, the social upheaval of the 1960s did not result from an empty value relativism nor from a wholesale rejection of moral authority. Rather, at its most serious and most troubling level, it evolved out of

---

*The approach to moral philosophy described here is developed by Michael Walzer in his 1987 book, *Interpretation and Social Criticism*.

conflicting interpretations of the traditions which inform Western notions of moral authority, as well as disputes over the appropriate character of moral authority in a democracy.

Such conflicts are poignantly characterized by King's question regarding those Christians who opposed the freedom movement: "Who is their God?" This question stems not from an intellectual concern over the existence of a deity who condones racism, but rather from an existential encounter with those who claim allegiance to such a deity. Whether or not this god exists outside of the attitudes and behaviors of those who claim allegiance to the god may be a matter for endless theological/philosophical speculation and of interest to some. But it is not an important matter for those, such as King, who are directly and often violently affected by the attitudes and behaviors of the believers. The vital concerns are rather how to be taken seriously as human beings of equal worth and dignity by such persons, and how to alter the cultural conditions which have precluded this possibility in the past.

The character of these vital concerns is at once moral, social and political. While many philosophers argue that such concerns cannot be addressed unless an objective and universal foundation for moral authority is first established, this approach tends to draw attention away from the immediate and concrete reality of those persons suffering now as a direct consequence of the attitudes and behaviors of those who claim to have already established such grounds for moral authority. Regardless of whether God, Reason, or Human Nature is presented as the locus for such authority, the same difficulties exist. While each of these foundations may support just and humane social arrangements, each may also—especially when absolutized at the center of a closed system—provide the justification for oppression and exploitation. Thus a thoughtful evaluation indicates that if moral philosophy is to be alive and genuinely concerned with the concrete lives of human beings, it must be situated squarely in the complex world of experience, history, and politics.

Moral absolutists who point to God, Reason, or an external Human Nature as the locus of moral authority will of course vehemently reject this understanding, claiming that it results in an empty relativism of values and a crisis for democracy evidenced most clearly by the chaotic rebellion of the 1960s. Yet, King and those he inspired can hardly be labeled as relativists, and the issue of whether "creative extremism" presents democracy with a desperate crisis or with a "constructive . . . tension which is necessary for growth" does not lend itself to resolution once and for all.

As was the case with those "Christians" whose racist attitudes and behaviors bewildered him so much, Martin Luther King, Jr. was situated within a history which shaped his experience and led him to interpret in certain ways various competing visions of moral authority present within the traditional materials available to him. Furthermore, neither King's experience nor the history which helped to shape that experience can be decontextualized from issues of power and politics. Any discussion of moral authority and democracy in which either concept is abstracted from the experiences and histories of the participants is, to employ a description coined by John Dewey, "irrelevant and doomed."

Here it may be helpful to compare in some detail two distinctive cultural traditions which inform Western notions of moral authority. The first—to which Allan Bloom claims primary allegiance—has its roots in the works of Plato, especially *The Republic*. The second—which stands in marked contrast to the Platonic tradition in moral orientation—is expressed most clearly in the books of the Hebrew prophets and is the tradition to which Martin Luther King, Jr. appealed most fully.

The issue of moral authority and the necessity of forming desirable attitudes and behaviors among citizens of the ideal state are at the center of Plato's *Republic*. Thus it is not surprising that a major concern for Socrates and his pupils is the divine image which will be permitted in the educational materials made available to the future guardians of the state. Plato's Socrates is not concerned with proving the existence of God, but he is quite sensitive to the ways in which images of the divine affect the attitudes and behaviors of persons. The young potential guardians must not, Socrates tells Adeimantus, "take into their souls opinions for the most part opposite to those we'll suppose they must have when they are grown up" (377b). For this reason, the poetic images of "what gods and heroes are like" must be consistent with models determined by the founders of the city. When Adeimantus asks what these appropriate models are, Socrates responds that "the god must surely always be described such as he is" (379a). To which, the almost ever-obliging Adeimantus simply replies, "Of course."

What follows from this point might be described as both theological rationalism and propaganda formulation. The eternal and thoroughly good nature of the god(s) is rationally determined, and the necessity of censoring any poetic representation which does not concur with this orthodoxy is agreed upon. Acceptable models of representation are developed. For example, when humans are punished by the god in a poet's tale, it must be because they (the humans) "needed punishment and . . . in paying the penalty they were benefited by the god" (380b). The god, however, is not all-powerful, but rather eternally capable *only* of good. For "the bad things, some other causes must be sought" (379a). Lastly, the god "will not lie, either in speech or deed" (382a).

The pedagogical purpose of this divine image is to nurture within the guardians certain attitudes and behaviors, in the interest of guaranteeing a harmonious social order. While Socrates is not explicit in this section about the content of the desired attitudes and behaviors, he does conclude that the aim is to make the guardians "god-fearing and divine insofar as a human being can possibly be" (383c). While this appears to be a noble end, its practical implications are ambiguous and problematic—even, as it turns out, for Socrates himself. For example, the duty of the philosopher-king, chosen from among the ranks of the guardians (the most god-like humans) is to preserve the stability and security of the ideal city. For this end, he is extended a considerable degree of latitude—in fact, far more latitude than the god whose image has informed his attitudes and behaviors. While the god "is altogether simple and true in deed and speech and doesn't change or deceive others by

illusions [or] speeches" (382c), the philosopher-king may lie
for the benefit of the state's stability whenever he deems it
appropriate.

And how is this contradictory action justified? How will
the philosopher-king's fellow citizens be convinced that their
ruler's most ungodly behavior is nonetheless good and just?
For this, Socrates—although not without some trepidation—must resort to myth-making in the form of the famous
"noble lie." That the social arrangement of the city is the
consequence of a metaphysical order is the lie needed to
maintain the authority of the philosopher-king and the stability of the state. This lie is reinforced by the divine image
which is to be allowed in the city, for it is the god who
fashions the rulers (by mixing in gold at their birth), and the
other lesser citizens (by mixing in iron, bronze, or silver).
Since the god—"such as he is"—can do *only* good, the resulting social order is good.

The irreverent democrat, I. F. Stone, once speculated as
to the fate of a citizen who would dare to contradict an
official lie spoken by the philosopher-king. Certainly Plato's
Socrates knows that once the social status quo is established, it must be protected. Educational indoctrination is
but the most subtle means of ensuring stability. But, interestingly, it is this very indoctrination which may prove problematic. While Socrates is committed to the pedagogical and
political end of devotion to the polis, his awareness that god
images must be controlled indicates also his cognizance of
the potency of such images in the lives of persons. Might an
unexpected consequence of the approved divine image be
that a young person so internalized the value of true speech
as to clash with an official lie? And even if this same young
person had internalized a commitment to the city's harmonious order, wouldn't a certain tension inevitably result?
Should this tension be articulated and sympathized with by
others, what action would be taken by the philosopher-king?
As Stone indicates, a society which values its own harmonious and stable existence above anything else must deal
quickly and often harshly with those who threaten that or-

der, and Plato's Socrates suggests any number of prescriptions for those whose presence in some way threatens the "perfect city." If a just society is synonymous with an orderly, stable, and rigidly hierarchical society, then any means of preservation are acceptable.

The notion of moral authority which stems from the Platonic tradition is alive and well in Western culture in these waning years of the twentieth century. It is, for example, the notion which informs Allan Bloom's concept of education for democracy, and the popular reception of his book (*The Closing Of The American Mind*) indicates that many share his understandings. This notion links moral authority with timeless and objective standards; those who reason best can know these standards, primarily through a process of discovery, and others should submit to their wisdom. This points to Plato's vision of the ideal social arrangement, a vision which continues to inform attitudes toward political life in the modern West.

This prescription for the ideal society is, of course, never completely filled—although history is replete with totalitarian attempts to fulfill it. Nor surprisingly, for Plato himself, the social arrangement which least resembles the ideal is a democracy, wherein opinion and passion—not reason—rule. Furthermore, when the *Crito* and the *Apology* are considered alongside of the *Republic,* a fatal set of social/political alternatives becomes apparent. Those who reason best must either use a combination of indoctrination and force to keep the masses in line or submit themselves to the jealous passions and unjust laws of the demos. Socrates, of course, ultimately chooses the latter option, claiming loyalty to the state which orders his execution. The possibility of persuading his fellow citizens to change the laws "in accordance with universal justice" is mentioned, but only in passing. This possibility is never seriously developed. Thus, Plato's notion of moral authority has two parts: the timeless and objective standards which are discernible to those who reason best and the legitimate sovereignty of the state over its citizens. The ideal political arrangement is a happy blend of these two components, but obedience to the state in the interest of social stability is essential regardless of the viability of the ideal.

Richard Rorty has observed that the "coalescence of reality and knowability" which characterizes the Western quest for philosophical/scientific certainty has its roots in Plato's "principle that only what is a matter of knowledge, rather than opinion, is fully real" ("Cartesian" 251). This objectivism, combined with Plato's utopian social vision, contributes to a notion of moral authority that many contemporary thinkers (a number of whom will be discussed in the following chapters of this study) see as pernicious when it comes to democratic social life. Given Plato's explicit contempt for Athenian democracy, this is hardly surprising. What is surprising is that the notion continues to pervade the attitudes and behaviors of so many "democrats" two and one-half millennia after Plato articulated it—contributing, for example, to biological determinism (which Stephen Jay Gould calls the "scientific version of Plato's tale" [20]). While many argue that this continuing influence results from the "greatness" of Plato's vision, others contend that its longevity is the consequence of the power of those whose interests are served by the vision and the entrenched cultural patterns supported by it. As will become apparent in following chapters, one's stance in relation to this issue profoundly influences one's normative concepts of democracy, and education for democracy.

The continuing influence of the Platonic notion of moral authority and the difficulties associated with it are evident in the attitudes and behaviors of those who opposed, either violently or passively, the civil rights movement of the 1960s, and in the attitudes and behaviors of those, including Martin Luther King, who advocated the movement. The claim that moral absolutes exist in nature was presented on both sides to justify social and political projects which stood in stark opposition to one another. In addition, as King's Birmingham letter so eloquently shows, the idea that God is the source of moral authority was endorsed on both sides of the civil rights debate. Obviously, then, what is taken as natural law or the will of God is influenced not only by one's history, but also by one's interests and intentions. Those who recognize this are not necessarily value relativists. Many such thinkers simply point out the existence of conflicting interpretations of the traditions which inform moral authority, and call into radical question the appropriateness of the Platonic tradition in relation to the need for citizens of a democracy to work together to create justice. These thinkers realize that Platonic "Truth" has too often been employed as a weapon against those who strove only to be acknowledged as human beings of equal worth and dignity and who challenged the authority of existing institutions which claimed the sanction of a natural or divine order.

Importantly, those who recognize the inadequacy of the Platonic tradition in relation to democracy often point to other understandings of moral authority available in Western cultural tradition, understandings which contain moral absolutes, and yet posit them with a keen awareness of human fallibility and the openness of history. Consider, for example, the case of the Hebrew prophets. Like the god image sanctioned by Socrates, the god of the prophets is good and just. But these terms take on altogether different meanings in the prophetic tradition. For the prophets, Yahweh's goodness and justice are characterized most fully by an ultimate compassion. In other words, Yahweh experiences what Abraham Joshua Heschel refers to as "divine pathos" in response to the suffering of human beings. The prophet's god is not omnipotent, but often stands powerless in the face of human evil, an evil which is manifested in the absence of goodness and justice, or—stated another way—in the human failure to experience and practice compassion.

Human beings thus fall short of the prophetic image of goodness, which is symbolized in the image of Yahweh as a supremely compassionate god. Moreover, although Yahweh's compassion is for all of creation, it is described most fully in relation to socially degraded persons—the poor, the afflicted, widows, orphans, strangers. Yahweh's perfect compassion thus sets the standard for justice and entails the basis for social criticism. In other words, the society of Israel is judged by the prophets as just or unjust depending on its sensitivity and response to human degradation, its compassion for the powerless. Furthermore, and importantly, justice and compassion are described in relation to the bodily reality of human beings, the need for food, clothing, shelter, which is inseparable from a central concern for human value and dignity.

Several specific demands of Yahweh are spelled out in Leviticus 25, which has to do with the material character of the Israelite society. Each person is to have the security of land and family. Slavery is forbidden, and persons who meet with misfortune are to be maintained by the community with gifts of food and interest-free loans. In no instance is human misfortune to be exploited for profit. This social and moral orientation is basic to the prophetic tradition; whenever Israelite society deviated from the norms presented in Leviticus 25, the prophet's voice was raised in protest.

In addition to voicing Yahweh's moral demands, the prophets insist on his supreme value in relation to all that is human. No idea, person, or society stands above Yahweh, and to attempt to do so is to commit idolatry, the worst of sins. (Contrary to what is often assumed, idolatry is not merely the formal worship of another god; rather it is a way of life which flouts prophetic standards of equality and compassion.) All that is human is subordinate to Yahweh and *only* to Yahweh; all are equal in this relationship, and all are obligated by virtue of it. Therefore, when the kings of Israel begin to interpret their status as "messiah" or as god's "chosen" in a way that positions their own importance above other persons, and therefore above Yahweh as well, disaster is imminent. When the rich "trample upon the needy . . . and buy the poor for silver" (Amos 8:4–6), the society has failed its moral obligation, and when "wise men" glory in their wisdom but fail to practice compassion, "what wisdom is there in them?" (Jer. 8:9)

Like the god image conceived in *The Republic* by Plato's Socrates, the prophetic god is a character with a role to play in society. But with respect to the notion of a script and author, important differences are apparent. For Socrates, the script is written by Nature, which prescribes the behavior of both humans and the gods. Insofar as humans can reason correctly (which only a select few can), the script—and thus reality—can be known. For the prophets, there is no script, or at least it does not exist in nature, but rather in history, as Yahweh and human beings interact, against a backdrop of covenant, yet both in their freedom. It is thus open-ended and subject to change. Within this major difference lie two very diverse concepts of moral authority. The Platonic concept depends on the capacity of human reason to grasp a natural and therefore universal reality; thus, the development of an epistemology which itself springs from the nature of things is presupposed. Only within this context can justice be defined, and this, of course, is what Socrates and his friends set out to do in *The Republic*. After justice is defined in this way, it can be actualized in the social and political world only if those who reason best manage the masses through a combination of force, indoctrination, and deception. For the prophets, on the other hand, moral authority has little if anything to do with the natural world and everything to do with the human world of history. In other words, prophetic justice is not something discovered by the few and imposed on the unsuspecting many. Rather, the prophets understand morality as a historical phenomenon, a social possession, and justice as the outcome of collective praxis—an endeavor informed by memory and hope.

Whitehead's famous observation that Western philosophy "consists of a series of footnotes to Plato" points to the domination exercised over modern sensibilities by the Platonic tradition. At the same time, however, modern social consciousness is shot through with what Cornel West calls "prophetic fragments." As indicated above, these two traditions support very different conceptions of moral authority, and even of democracy itself. Shared in common by both traditions, however, is a sense of crisis in relation to the health of liberal democracy. Because one's normative conception of democracy determines one's normative conception of education, this sense of crisis is often articulated as a critique of the values manifested in academia. Both Platonic and prophetic thinkers, for example, deplore (and discuss in a language of "crisis") the lack of authority enjoyed by *any* cultural tradition in today's technocratic academic settings and fear that without a vital sense of connectedness to the past, today's students lack the critical sensibilities needed to participate judiciously and effectively in an increasingly complex future. This point of consensus, however, is itself highly ambiguous because Platonic and prophetic thinkers differ radically on what it means to "participate judiciously and effectively" in the interest of democracy. These differences and their implications for democratic social life are discussed in the following chapters.

In today's colleges and universities, much modern philosophy continues in the Platonic tradition, perceiving itself, as Stephen Toulmin puts it, "as the pure product of a reflective mind untouched by external events" (56). But this perception has been challenged repeatedly throughout the last century, and the notions of moral authority which accompany the modern mind-set have also been thrown into radical question. Three major sources of this challenge have been Continental hermeneutics, feminism,and the "home-grown" philosophy of American pragmatism.

In the past decade, a variety of hybrid philosophies integrating themes from these three sources have evolved. These hybrids, such as the "democratic-socialist-feminist-pragmatism" of Nancy Fraser and the "prophetic pragmatism" of Cornel West (both of which will be discussed in following pages), propose new theoretical approaches to moral life, approaches more conducive to democratic community. To varying degrees, all of these new proposals are consistent in spirit with both prophetic morality and the philosophical project of John Dewey, whose own attempt was to articulate a moral philosophy in the interest of what he called "creative democracy."

Dewey's work contains a particular vision of the appropriate character of moral authority in a democracy, a vision which is inseparable from his unique faith in education as a nurturer of reflective intelligence and of social responsibility. Although he does not situate his vision within any par-

ticular religious tradition, it is fair to say that Dewey's notion of creative democracy has far more in common with
prophetic sensibilities than with Platonic ones. (The religious framework from which he emerged—liberal, evange-
lical Congregationalist—cannot be ignored here, anymore
than can be King's experience in the prophetic black church.)
For Dewey, as for the prophets, morality is a social possession and history is open-ended. While he does not appeal to
the moral authority of tradition and in fact makes it clear
that there is no "voice so authoritative as to preclude the
need of inquiry," Dewey recognizes the "fact" that humans
are born "organic beings associated with others" (*The Public
and Its Problems* 154). In other words, humans are social
beings by nature. Thus, Dewey's claim that morality is social
is descriptive; insofar as morality exists, it does so because
"we live in a world where other persons live too" (*Human
Nature and Conduct* 326). As with all knowledge, then, our
understanding of moral authority "depends upon tradition,
upon tools and methods socially-transmitted, developed and
sanctioned" (*Public* 158). But just as cultural tradition informs our notions of goodness and justice, we create tradition by means of reflective intelligence and participation in
the development of a shared culture.

All of this does not mean that participation in the creation of democratic culture is a given—far from it. Freedom
and equality, in Dewey's sense, are not natural possessions,
except as they exist potentially. As opposed to the theories of
classical Liberalism (which inherit from the Greeks a framework of metaphysical givens which translate into "self-evident" truths), Dewey argues that genuine freedom cannot be
defined "on the basis of something antecedently given"
("Philosophies" 200). Rather, freedom requires "favorable
objective conditions," social institutions which effectively
promote its actualization. Freedom is thus an achievement,
something which comes to be only if it is actively and collec-
tively nurtured. Dewey's understanding of equality is similar. Equality, in his sense, is equality of participation and "in
the consequences of associated action." It is not a natural
possession; rather, equality is the fruit of a community

which values and actively (self-consciously) seeks it for all of its members.

For Dewey, traditional notions of moral authority have involved all the errors of "individualistic psychology." Put another way, Western philosophy since Socrates has developed within a frame of reference which presupposes both individual "mind" and a direct link between individual consciousness and the eternal, universal truths contained in Nature. Our notions of what it means to be human and of what it means to live in community have been informed—with unfortunate consequences, in Dewey's estimation—by this pretheoretical frame of reference. This basic paradigmatic error is precisely what Dewey attempted to correct (or at least avoid) because he believed that the future of democracy depended on just such a paradigm shift. In many ways, then, to use Cornel West's rather shocking term, Dewey "evaded" philosophy and attempted instead to define and nurture the social and cultural conditions under which both democratic political judgment and democratic political practice could flourish.

If this reading of Dewey is correct, then his vision is alive today in the works of such individuals as Cornel West, Richard J. Bernstein and Benjamin Barber, as well as an increasing number of feminist thinkers whose ideas are only beginning to challenge entrenched institutionalized notions of the "private" and "public." As Dewey well knew, to philosophize is to engage in political praxis, and his own political vision is writ large in his philosophy. That vision is of a piece with Benjamin Barber's understanding of political judgment and democratic citizenship.

> The citizen wishes . . . only to act rightly, not to know for certain; . . . only to overcome conflict and secure transient peace, not to discover eternity; only to cooperate with others, not to achieve moral oneness; only to formulate common causes, not to obliterate all differences. Politics is what [humans] do when metaphysics fails. . . . It is the forging of common actuality in the absence of abstract, independent standards . . . and it is feasible only when in-

dividuals are transformed by social interaction into citizens. (*Conquest* 209)

Barber continues:

The secret of political judgment is neither to discover absolute standards by which the wise might take measure of political justice nor to refine the mental faculties of the citizenry by teaching them philosophy so that they might emulate the wise. It is rather to inform their discretion and enlarge their political experience. A citizenry in action, capable of thinking as a "we" in the name of public goods, is about as much political judgment—for better or worse—as humankind is likely to be permitted. (211)

Barber's concern for a community of citizens with a "well-developed capacity for political judgment" points to his definition of democracy as a form of human relations and harks back to Dewey's own definition: "a way of life . . . which [requires] the participation of every mature human being in formation of the values that regulate the living of [persons] together" (*Problems of Men* 57). This basic understanding of democracy entails rejection of the Platonic notion that those individuals who reason best must either use a combination of indoctrination and force to manage the masses or submit themselves to the ugly whims of those who cannot reason at all. Both Barber and Dewey recognize that when judgment is subsumed under reason, and reason is defined as a process of individual consciousness, the concept of political participation is impoverished. The moral authority of "philosophers" or "experts" is posited as prior to that of reflective citizens, and the consequence is what Dewey calls "a subtle form of suppression." When this suppression is "habitual and embodied in social institutions, it seems the normal and natural state of affairs," and the *experience* of democracy, which is vital to the development of political judgment, is so restricted as to preclude the very possibility of democracy (*Problems* 58). As Barber puts it, "[P]olitical judgment is something produced by politics rather than by cognition; its concomitant is citizenship rather than individual consciousness" (*Conquest* 203).

Thus it is apparent that both Dewey and Barber may be situated in a tradition in which the value of a rich democratic human connectedness takes precedence over the value of philosophical Truth. One—and arguably the major—source for this tradition, as indicated above, is the collected works of the Hebrew prophets. The affinity between prophetic and democratic sensibilities is poignantly affirmed in Elie Wiesel's declaration that "Jewish theology is human relations," and the connection is made even more fully explicit in the works of Cornel West, which will be discussed at some length in chapters 5 and 6 of this book.

In the preface to Barber's *Strong Democracy,* he writes that his aim is to "find an approach to democracy suitable to human relations rather than to truth." I have drawn from Barber to describe my own task in this book: to situate in political context the humanities crisis in general and the crisis of Western philosophy in particular, and to seek an approach to liberal education suitable to the relational character of "strong" and "creative" democracy. This task is at once concerned with conflicting interpretations of the traditions which inform Western notions of moral authority and with disputes over the appropriate character of moral authority in a democracy. Furthermore, it presupposes a prophetic concern for those who are socially degraded, those who struggle to be taken seriously as human beings of equal worth and dignity, and who seek ways of altering the cultural conditions which have precluded this possibility in the past. I have approached this task by surveying in dialectical fashion the views of several contemporary and fairly prominent North American academic humanists and by analyzing their philosophical positions in relation to "creative democracy."

While I have tried to present these conflicting philosophical positions as fairly and honestly as possible, I do not understand myself as an objective or disinterested observer of the ideological debates described in these pages. The intellectual and moral community with which I identify is

committed to what Sharon Welch calls "the practice of com-
municative ethics" (*Ethic of Risk* 123ff.) and the concomitant
understanding voiced by Jane Addams that "unless all [per-
sons] contribute to a good, we cannot even be sure that it is
worth having" (Cremin, *Transformation* ix). This ethical
sensibility has implications both for one's relation to historical tradition and for the politics of everyday life.

For example, while the prophetic tradition is one that I
find largely consistent with the ethical spirit of Welch and
Addams, I am also sympathetic with another feminist concern—expressed eloquently by Carol Christ—that a strain of
violence, intolerance, and exclusivity is embedded within
this ancient tradition. This point of ambivalence illustrates
my experience of the vast complexity of interpretation and
the intricacy of my own existential relation to tradition. In
one sense, the prophets did fall miserably short of the ideal
of pluralism. In fact, they may be understood as the ancient
epitome of "political correctness." But that label is as problematic when it comes to the prophets as it is when applied
today. Prophetic intolerance, in its best (but perhaps not its
only) sense, came in response to any form of systematic
oppression. Furthermore, the prophets gave a voice to the
marginalized members of their society insofar as it was possible within an ancient patriarchal setting; indeed they were
themselves marginalized. Thus, for those who occupy a similar position in relation to modern patriarchal society, the
prophets can indeed provide a model for ethical resistance.
This does not mean that the prophetic tradition is immune
to critique. It simply means that one can be sustained by the
spirit of the tradition while recognizing that it is flawed,
unfinished, and in need of "challenge, renewal and reconstruction" (Brown 208).

This stance in relation to tradition is consistent with
Dewey's notion of "creative democracy," and with Robert
McAfee Brown's claim that "a moral society will be perpetually unfinished" (208). For Sharon Welch, the perpetual
creation of a good society requires not only "dialogue with
actual members of different communities," but also prior
material interaction—defined as "either political conflict or

coalition or joint involvement in life-sustaining work"—for the fruition of that dialogue (*Ethic of Risk* 124).

My study assumes that institutions of higher education are one vital setting for the material interaction and meaningful dialogue seen by Welch as necessary for the creation of a moral society. In these settings today, intelligent, decent, and well-meaning persons disagree radically over the meaning of the "good" in relation to democracy and education for democracy. These persons draw upon different traditions, histories, and experiences to confirm their own visions of the moral society. They represent different moral communities. The vital challenge for these persons, as Barber puts it, is to develop the capacity to think of a "we" in the name of common goods, while maintaining their diversity and particularity.

The ideological conflicts which characterize liberal education today may be seen as a microcosm of those which characterize contemporary U.S. society. Furthermore, many indications point to potentially greater ideological contestation. In recent months, for example, professional and popular publications have repeatedly reminded us of the changing demographics of Western society. *Time Magazine,* for example, predicts that by 2056, the "average" U.S. citizen will "trace his or her descent to Africa, Asia, the Hispanic world, the Pacific Islands, Arabia—almost anywhere but white Europe" (9 April 1990). Such increasing cultural diversity points to the ever more pressing need for a thorough examination of the pretheoretical frames of reference which have informed Western notions of humanistic scholarship, particularly philosophy and history, and of the political dimensions of that scholarship. What some critics have labeled as the "crisis" of the humanities is actually the attempt of many scholars to begin such an examination. As John Trimbur puts it, "The normative meaning in question [in the humanities crisis] is the one that underlies Marlow's narrative in *Lord Jim*—what does it mean to be one of us?" (113)

This question, unfortunately, is not often stated with Trimbur's candor in the more highly publicized debates over humanities education. In fact, the political character of this question is denied by those who identify the "politicization" of the humanities as part of their crisis. This perception coheres with the traditional social mission of education, which is the maintenance—rather than the transformation—of existing social and economic structures. In light of our increasingly multicultural social reality and the ever more pressing need for new forms of democratic community, this mission must be radically critiqued. Such a critique entails an open acknowledgment of what is at stake, socially and politically, in the humanities debate; Trimbur's assessment and the question it contains are vital to this critique.

While the role of higher education as an agent of genuine cultural transformation is ambiguous, social change is inevitable. The question is whether or not our political judgment—our capacity to think of a "we" in the name of public goods—is sufficiently developed to chart a just and peaceful democratic course, or whether democracy will crumble under the weight of state-corporate institutions so entrenched and so interconnected that democratic experience is precluded. Assuming that higher education can contribute to the development of democratic political judgment (and this is not, I confess, an assumption that I posit with the faith of John Dewey), the humanities present us with a vital opportunity, precisely because they exist at this moment in a state of conflict and tension. This tension—which is especially apparent in philosophy and history—serves not only as an occasion to rethink the appropriate character of moral authority in a democracy, it provides a significant trial for that institution most closely associated with the values of creative democracy. Moreover, the way in which these conflicts are resolved—or not resolved—may well be a harbinger of the character of social and political life "beyond the melting pot."

Introduction: The Crisis in Humanities Education and Liberal Democracy: Three Views

Education implies teaching. Teaching implies knowledge. Knowledge is truth. The truth is everywhere the same. Hence education should be everywhere the same.

—Robert Hutchins

Universality is when we take shit forever, with smiles on our faces.

—Sam Greenlee

Repeatedly throughout the past decade the message has been announced: liberal education, particularly the humanities, is in crisis. The discourse or rhetoric of crisis has come from a variety of diverse sources, from the political Left as well as the Right, from academic humanists, administrators, bureaucrats, and the popular press. For students of twentieth-century educational history, much of the discourse seems reminiscent of the 1930s, when John Dewey and Robert Hutchins and their respective disciples debated in often heated terms the appropriate content and character of liberal education. But anyone with even passing familiarity with the views of these two giant North American educational philosophers recognizes that neither man won

1

the day. On one hand, the growing emphasis on business
and science has resulted in academic programs in which the
humanities—the core of Hutchin's liberal arts vision—are
increasingly marginalized. On the other hand, charges of
ethnocentrism, racism, and sexism haunt the traditional
liberal arts curriculum, which is castigated for its DEWM
(Dead European White Male) bias. Thus it appears that the
"barriers of class, race, and national territory" which Dewey
wanted broken down in the interest of genuine democracy
are still firmly entrenched (*Democracy and Education* 87).
The humanities, then, have been nudged from a central
position in the undergraduate general education curricula
while also being torn from within by radical disagreements
over their content and character. Perceived in this light,
what Hutchins described in 1953 as "the conflict in education" seems bound to have developed into "crisis" sooner or
later.

One need not search at great length to gather documen-
tary evidence of the humanities' special crisis. Controversial
attempts abound nationwide to revise and reform undergraduate curricula. A multitude of committees, commis-
sions, and free-lance experts have devoted endless hours
and issued scores of reports for the purpose of defining
what's wrong with liberal education. And most of these reports point to the "lack [of] meaningful coherence, cohesion,
and continuity" in the humanities (West, Introduction, *Hermeneutics* 67). The crisis is even reflected in the financial
community. For example, in 1988 came the bewildering
news that Citibank officials had instituted a policy (deemed
altogether legal by their attorneys) which denied credit to
humanities majors strictly on the basis of their "field of
study" (Chang, *The National College Newspaper,* September
1988, 14). This despite the claim of many business leaders
that the humanities prepare students for lucrative careers
in the commercial world.

A recent indication of the status of the humanities at
land grant universities is Iowa State University's Public
Policy Education Project, a program implemented to "put
Iowa leaders in touch with the most current, relevant, and

understandable information regarding the major issues" facing the state (PPEP Pamphlet). While a campuswide committee of directors was established for the project, not a single humanities scholar, not even a philosopher or historian, was among them. When queried as to the reason for this omission, the project coordinator replied with, I believe, genuine regret, that it had to do with "historical institutional barriers."

In all of the above examples, radical doubts are apparent, not only as to what the humanities *are,* but also what they are *for* and what they are *good for* in the social and political world of the late twentieth century. This, in turn, points to a problematic popular image and professional self-image of the humanist intellectual. As literary critic Frank Lentricchia puts it:

> The popular conception of the humanist . . . is that *he* is
> the sort of male who is not now, nor ever will be, in danger
> of penetrating the social texture of his time. His ideas are
> not now, nor ever will be, in danger of inseminating everyday life. ("The 'Life' " 27)

Gerald Graff and Jerry Herron concur with Lentricchia. As Graff observes in the foreword to Herron's 1988 book *Universities and the Myth of Cultural Decline:*

> In a society which classifies [the humanities] under the
> Sunday supplement category "Arts and Leisure," there is
> no need to worry about [humanistic] intellectual culture
> becoming subordinated to instrumental ends. It is not
> thought to have any. (9)

Both Graff and Herron argue that the contemporary humanities are reaping the confusion sown throughout their history. On one hand, the humanities were represented, by Cardinal Newman for example, as an end to themselves: humanities for humanities' (or in some rather vague sense, humanity's) sake. Any notion of vulgar utility was—and for the most part, continues to—abhorrent. On the other hand, as Graff and Herron argue, at the very moment of this representation (mid-nineteenth century), humanistic education was a "prerequisite to the professions and to positions of national leadership" (10). Thus, the humanities actually "owe their inherited educational and social prestige to the fact that they have not existed in a disinterested realm, but have directly contributed to the middle class world of work and success" (10). But this world has changed. In an age of "technocratic capitalism," familiarity with humanistic intellectual culture is not needed to assure or legitimate social success and, in fact, may work against it.

One key question thus becomes apparent: What role do the humanities play in relation to the social and political world of the late twentieth century? Many thinkers—those of a conservative or reactionary bent—look with nostalgia to a time when humanistic intellectual culture commanded prestige and exercised social authority. The thesis advocated by Graff and Herron supports this perspective. The difference is that conservative thinkers, such as William Bennett and Allan Bloom, resist the notion that the humanities' prestige and authority waned as a consequence of social and economic developments outside of academic humanities departments. They maintain that the deterioration of the humanities' authority in contemporary society has been self-induced by humanist intellectuals who have forsaken their own tradition and now languish in a swamp of relativism and nihilism. Furthermore, conservative thinkers concur that the contemporary crisis of the humanities is intrinsically related to the failing health of liberal democracy, which needs the philosophical authority of Truth and Reason to survive.

Chapters 1 and 2 of this book are an analysis of the conservative discourse of crisis, especially that of Allan Bloom, and to a critique of this discourse. These chapters thus set the stage and manifest the dialectical approach taken throughout this study to the issues at hand. For example, the ideas of neo-pragmatist philosopher Richard Rorty, whose critique of the conservative view is discussed in chapter 2, are explored far more fully in chapter 3.

Rorty, it should be noted, does not refer to a crisis in higher education, but he does argue that his liberal-pragmatic conception of the humanities is more conducive to democracy than is the conservative conception. Rorty believes that a rejection of philosophical realism (which Bloom sees as the only genuine philosophy) is necessary for genuine democratic solidarity. The task for the humanities, he argues, is to help create a language (and thus a culture) in which "our finite and contingent sense of human community" would replace the authority of God and/or Reason ("Hermeneutics" 6). This is essential for liberal democracy because inculcating a sense of community entails charging that community with the responsibility of "choosing its own destiny" (6). Thus, for Rorty, the humanities do—or *should*—serve a social purpose, but importantly, this purpose has only poetic, not philosophically authoritative, grounds. From Rorty's perspective, this is no denial of the humanities' importance. In fact, Rorty's controversial project throughout the past decade has been to show that *all* intellectual endeavor, including science, is historically and linguistically contingent. Like Dewey, then, Rorty advocates erasing the traditional lines separating the "two cultures" and viewing all intellectual endeavor as a creation of metaphors for reality, not as a discovery of reality.

As might be expected, Rorty has managed to provoke criticism from both his political left and right. Having already explored the views of his conservative rivals, I will continue my dialectical study in chapter 4 by examining the general critique of Rorty which emanates from his political left. In the following chapter, I will analyze in more detail the ideas of one of Rorty's radical critics, Cornel West.

Interestingly, West's radical discourse of crisis shares some common ground with that articulated by political conservatives. Like the latter, West laments the isolation, self-doubt, and diminished authority of the humanities; but, unlike the conservatives, West does not attribute the humanities crisis to the philosophical and cultural relativism of contemporary academic humanists. Rather, West affirms with Rorty the historical and linguistic contingency of all intellectual endeavor. But unlike Rorty, West maintains that one cannot historicize humanistic intellectual culture without politicizing it. The upshot, then, is that West situates the humanities crisis in both historical and political context. He argues that without a critical awareness of the social injustice and political brutality which surround and even permeate the academy, one cannot substantively critique the "debased and debilitating isolation . . . professionalization, and specialization" which characterize the academic humanities, and which define their contemporary crisis.

Like Bloom and Rorty, West maintains that his approach to humanistic intellectual culture is vital to the future of *democracy*. Thus the meaning of what Carl Sandburg called that "great, strange, holy word" becomes itself a central issue in the controversy surrounding the humanities, at least as exemplified by these three scholars. West's conception differs radically from that of either Bloom or Rorty and prompts him to incorporate the elements of "Afro-American critical thought" (the prophetic tradition, pragmatism, and progressive Marxism) into "prophetic pragmatism," a form of cultural criticism aimed at "promoting . . . creative democracy by means of critical intelligence and social action" (*Evasion* 212).

West's reference to "creative democracy" is an allusion to "Creative Democracy: The Task Before Us," an essay written by John Dewey for a 1939 conference celebrating his eightieth birthday. I began this study with a vague awareness that its themes would hark back to the concerns which preoccupied Dewey for all of his adult life. By the time I completed it, I had developed a monumental respect for North America's "philosopher of democracy." In the words of Antonio Gramsci, Dewey was a genuine "organic intellectual," one who took the life of the mind seriously enough to relate his ideas to the social realities of his day and who interpreted and critiqued cultural tradition through an engagement with the experiences of those who were socially degraded in a country which claimed to epitomize the values of freedom and equality. By so doing, Dewey showed that democracy is far from a *fait accompli*. It is rather a "tradition which has not yet become."

Not surprisingly, a majority of the thinkers surveyed in this text draw upon the work of Dewey. Along with, and to no small degree *because* of him, they recognize that creative democracy is still "the task before us."

CHAPTER ONE

The Conservative Discourse of Crisis in the 1980s

Introduction

In 1982, writing in *Harvard Magazine,* Walter Jackson Bate announced, "The humanities are not merely entering, they are plunging into their worst state of crisis since the modern university was formed a century ago" (46). Since its publication, Bate's article has been widely quoted, both by those who strongly agree with its message, conservatives such as William Bennett and Lynne Cheney, and by those who—for various reasons—strongly disagree, including Paul de Man, Jacques Derrida, and Stanley Fish (Jeffords 108). While Bate did not point directly to a link between the crisis of the humanities and the fate of Western democracy, his essay has been called upon to reinforce the arguments of Bennett and Cheney, who do make this link and who have held positions of visibility and authority in relation to humanities education in the past decade. Therefore, Bate's article provides a helpful background for the conservative position.

Walter Jackson Bate

Bate traces the crisis of the humanities to changes in the university brought about by the new scientific paradigm which originated in late nineteenth-century Germany.* This

---

*For thorough discussion of this transition, see Lilge's *The Abuse of Learning: The Failure of the German University* and McClelland's *State, Society, and University in Germany, 1700–1914.*

change from a classical curriculum which took for granted
the unity of knowledge to one committed to academic specialization based on the new understanding of science was
quickly emulated in the United States and resulted in frag-
mented and regimented departments which were soon accepted as the norm for university structure. The consequences of this transition were dire for the humanities, which
traditionally prided themselves on their concern with the
holistic experience of human beings. Furthermore, specialization led to the construction of esoteric vocabularies, each
associated with a particular "expert" knowledge, whereas
the language of the humanities from ancient Greece onward
was accessible to all readers.

According to Bate, as the humanities accommodated
themselves to the principle of specialization, they lost their
authority, identity, and purpose. Their claim of nurturing a
valuable way of knowing, their ideal of trusting the "moral
and educative effect . . . of knowledge" in relation to human
character, their dedication to synthesizing an "interplay of
mind and experience": all of these have been severely undermined by the humanities' submission to the scientific
paradigm. This submission was brought about, in part, by
the "seduction" of humanist scholars by formalistic theories
and methods congruent with the dominant scientific paradigm. Bate attributes this "seduction" to two "feelings
treacherously important to the human psyche: the yearning
for importance and the craving for safety" (49). In other
words, knowing more and more about less and less and
camouflaging what one does know in arcane language are
psychologically appealing in a culture which values only "the
authority of experts." Aggravating the psychological "seduction" of academic humanists were administrators who themselves had been indoctrinated by the scientific paradigm and
who thus equated "productivity" with the creation of "new"
knowledge and publication, both of which were measured
quantitatively.

Bate traces the various ills of specialization through the
twentieth century, concentrating primarily on his own field,
English, after 1955. From that time onward, he maintains,

a growing polarization has existed between traditional Renaissance humanists and new academic humanists (those "seduced" by specialization). Bate's sympathy, of course, is with the former, and he laments the latter group's increasing size and stature, as well as its general ignorance of the "legacy of thought and the inheritance of idealism" which is in danger of being forever lost.

At a certain time—Bate does not indicate when—an event occurred which accelerated the demise of the humanities: "the bottom fell out of the job-market, with a speed and completeness never before experienced" (50). Bate attributes this event to three causes: 1) the vast overproduction of Ph.D.'s—particularly at state universities which were especially guilty of turning out students who viewed "literature as a private preserve, and [who] were . . . innocent of history, of philology, of 'ideas' generally"; 2) inflation; and 3) public disillusionment with higher education. Furthermore, many of the Ph.D.'s who had emerged from state universities now had tenured teaching positions. The result was that humanities departments were paralyzed by inflation and public disillusion at the precise moment in which they were held in the tenured grip of those academics most likely to be "innocent of ideas," in other words, those state-university-educated Ph.D.'s who simply had not been "trained" to preserve the "civilization of the Logos."

When forced to justify the existence of their departments to administrations hard pressed for funding, the "new academic humanists" developed scores of new courses with the goal of attracting students who might otherwise have shunned the field. Women's Studies, ethnic literature and history, film classes, Business English: for Bate all of these represent the demise of the humanities. Meanwhile, the felt need for intellectual rigor has not completely diminished; unfortunately, however, it has led to philosophical and literary theories (structuralism, deconstruction) which tend to create for humanities scholarship a "separate preserve, apart from the common experience of life" (52).

What is left in the humanities is isolation, intellectual emptiness, and a "potentially suicidal movement among 'leaders of the profession'" (52). Without its traditional center of the Renaissance ideal, the humanities flounder, sprawl in "helpless disarray." Thus, the crisis of the humanities as defined by W. Jackson Bate.

William Bennett

Anyone familiar with the ideas of William Bennett (and given his visibility in the past decade, it is likely that many persons are familiar with his ideas) will readily understand why he has drawn upon Bate's *Harvard Magazine* article to reinforce his own conception of the humanities. Bennett's direct use of Bate is found in the 1984 NEH *Report on Humanities in Education (To Reclaim a Legacy)*, but only two months after the publication of Bate's article, Bennett wrote for the *Wall Street Journal* a piece entitled "The Shattered Humanities," in which one finds views quite similar to those of Bate. (This is not, of course, to suggest that Bate's article was the germ for Bennett's recognition of the humanities crisis, but only that the two men have related understandings.) However, while Bate attempts to locate the difficulties surrounding humanities education in at least limited historical context, Bennett flatly maintains in the *Wall Street Journal* that "the greatest threat to the humanities lies within." In other words, those who practice the academic humanities have "lost faith" in their own tradition, their own enterprise. They demonstrate what Bennett refers to as a "perverse embarrassment . . . about the achievements of our civilization." Furthermore, within the academic humanities, "there seems to be competition for complete unintelligibility," as "self-isolating vocabularies . . . abound within subdisciplines." The consequences of this inner decay is that the humanities have become—or are quickly becoming—"phony and empty," repelling students who are concerned with "matters of enduring importance . . . courage, fidelity, friendship, honor, love, justice, goodness, ambiguity, time, power, faith." (Note the departure from Bate's understanding that the "new humanities" developed as the result of the need to pander to a wider range of students, in order to justify the existence of humanities departments. Of course, it may be that Bennett is simply lamenting the character of the students drawn to the "new humanities," over against the character of those somehow repelled.)

Bennett's major statement on the humanities crisis is the aforementioned 1984 NEH report, *To Reclaim a Legacy*. Here, he maintains that the purpose of the humanities is to transmit to students a "common culture rooted in civilization's lasting vision, its highest shared ideals and aspirations, and its heritage" (17). In addition, he rejects the idea that this purpose is problematic in relation to developing a core curriculum given the pluralism of United States society, and he points instead to what he "suspects" is a "consensus on what the great books are" (18). He bases his suspicion on a "test" which was undertaken to determine "what the American public thinks are the most significant works." The test consisted of Bennett's invitation to "several hundred educational .and cultural leaders" and columnist George Will's identical invitation to his readers to submit lists of ten books that any high school graduate should have read. Out of the approximately five hundred responses to these invitations, over 50 percent agreed on four "texts and authors . . . Shakespeare's plays, American historical documents . . . *The Adventures of Huckleberry Finn,* and the Bible." The point to be gathered from this "test" is clear, maintains Bennett; there is "broader agreement on what the [most important] books are than many have supposed." Furthermore, he believes that this is as true at the college level as it is in secondary schools.

As to the drop in the number of humanities majors, Bennett returns to the theme of his *Wall Street Journal* text. The "conventional wisdom" which attributes declining student interest to the "concern for finding good-paying jobs after college" is not adequate (18). Rather, the failure is internal to the academy, which has failed to "bring the humanities to life and to insist on their value." Part of this failure is that of administrators who determine the allocation of resources, but named first by Bennett (in terms of failure allocation) are those who teach the humanities. The important factors contributing to the failure of humanities teachers are specialization, the relativism of values, and ideological bias (19).

Bennett's critique of specialization strongly resembles that of Bate, and thus I will not analyze it here. The other major factors contributing to the failure of humanities teachers—relativism and ideological bias—are on opposite ends of the same pole. On one hand, "the humanities are declared to have no inherent meaning because all meaning is subjective and relative to one's own perspective" (19). On the other hand, "some humanities professors" treat their disciplines as if they were "the handmaiden of ideology, subordinated to particular prejudices and valued or rejected on the basis of their relation to a certain social stance." The consequence is that students, put off by both approaches, have "stampeded out of humanities departments."

Bennett's prescription for the humanities is a return to an intellectually authoritative core curriculum to offset the relativism which now holds sway. He spurns curriculum developed on the basis of "political compromise" and proposes humanities classes which offer "the best that has been thought and written" to non-majors, as well as to majors. These steps, he believes, would put an end to narrow specialization, value relativism, and the ideological biases which undermine humanities education from within. Furthermore, because inheriting the intellectual legacy of Western civilization is a valuable right of every citizen, the humanities must be restored to their central place in the undergraduate curriculum (21).

In 1988—now writing as United States Secretary of Education—Bennett again picked up the gauntlet, this time to defend his view of the humanities in the wake of Stanford University's decision to revise its humanities requirements and to include courses in non-Western culture. In his syndicated column, "Collegiate Times," Bennett maintained that at stake in Stanford's decision was "more than the fate of a single requirement" ("Western Principles"). Rather, the issue of whether and why Western civilization courses should be kept at the core of the undergraduate curriculum points to the larger concern of the responsibility of education to *"nurture* and *defend"* the West (emphasis added). To the arguments for strong Western-centered humanities programs presented in his earlier NEH texts, Bennett adds two: 1) Western civilization "has set the moral, political, economic, and social standards for the rest of the world," and 2) "the West is under attack," most notably "from within."

In his strongest language thus far, Bennett (now borrowing explicitly from Allan Bloom) describes the Western principles of "freedom and equality" as defining "the universal standard of legitimacy." He points once again to the "perennial questions" debated within Western philosophy and literature and condemns those who "attack Western values and accomplishments." America, he maintains, has served and continues to serve as "a beacon to the world," and it is those who deny this—claiming "racism, imperialism, sexism, capitalism, ethnocentrism, elitism, and a host of other 'isms,'" who wish to diminish the study of the West in our colleges and universities.

Thus, while repeating many of Bate's arguments, Bennett adds his own particular slant, that of patriotism, and importantly, patriotism determined by one's conception of the humanities. In Bennett's view, to challenge the content and character of the traditional humanities is to be an enemy of freedom and equality. Furthermore, such "enemies" are located primarily "within" colleges and universities.

Lynne Cheney

Bennett's successor as chair of the National Endowment for the Humanities was Lynne Cheney, who compiled two major reports early in her tenure. The first, *American Memory,* is a study of the "state of the humanities" in elementary and secondary schools, which I will not explore here because my central concern is with higher education. However, while research for *American Memory* was in progress, Cheney spoke to the American Council of Learned Societies

(spring 1987) and included in her text the telling claim that
"since students are arriving on college campuses without
knowing what literature and history are, we shouldn't be
surprised that they don't think about majoring in them ("Defending" 38).

In March 1988, while researching her second major
NEH report (*Humanities in America*), Cheney assembled a
committee of "professors, writers, and publishers" to discuss
one of the report's sections, "The Scholar and Society" (Heller 4). The central topic addressed by this committee was the
relationship (or lack thereof) between humanities scholarship in the university and society at large. Once again, the
debate centered on specialization in the context of the humanities' traditional mission to speak in accessible language
to "common human concerns." This topic occupies much of
Humanities in America, which begins with a celebration of
the humanities in American life. In society as a whole, Cheney declares, the humanities are thriving. Historical associations, library reading programs, serious book sales, PBS
series shaped by "world-famed scholars": all of these and
more point to the "remarkable blossoming" of the humanities in the United States.

The tone of Cheney's report changes, however, when she
addresses the state of the humanities in colleges and universities. Quoting Bate, Cheney refers to the "disarray and
isolation . . . rupture and distrust . . . lost sense of meaning"
which characterize the academic humanities. To the familiar cries of "specialization" and "relativism," Cheney adds a
third, which is similar to Bennett's earlier discussion of patriotism. But rather than explicitly labeling those who challenge the traditional humanities' content and character as
"enemies" of freedom and equality, Cheney speaks disparagingly of those who "politicize" the humanities.

> Some scholars reduce the study of the humanities to the
> study of politics, arguing that truth—and beauty and ex-
> cellence—are not timeless matters, but transitory notions,
> devices used by some groups to perpetuate "hegemony"
> over others. These scholars call into question all intellec-

tual and aesthetic valuation, conceiving "the political perspective," in the words of one " . . . as the absolute horizon of all reading and interpretation" (*Humanities in America* 7).

This trend toward politicization detracts from the humanities' capacity to speak to "the deepest concerns we all have as human beings," to the questions perennially given rise by the "human condition" (8). Between specialization and politicization, the humanities are reduced to arcane subdisciplines which appeal only to an elite and isolated corps of academic intellectuals.

Furthermore, politicization complicates the already difficult task of "determining a substantive and coherent plan of study for undergraduates" (12). Cheney, like Bennett, rejects the idea that requiring a traditional Western core is equivalent to imposing an oppressive political consensus. Quoting Stanley Hook, who maintains that "Western culture has been most critical of itself," Cheney maintains that

[t]he humanities are about more than politics, about more than social power. What gives them their abiding worth are truths that pass beyond time and circumstance; truths that, transcending accidents of class, race, and gender, speak to us all. (14)

The Educational Philosophy Shared by Bate, Bennett, and Cheney

An analysis of the texts of Bate, Bennett, and Cheney suggests the fairly cohesive character of their approach to the humanities. Summarized, the views of these three thinkers are as follows: The humanities are in a crisis created primarily by those who teach them in colleges and universities. The crisis is characterized by 1) specialization, 2) relativism, and 3) politicization. Excessive *specialization* has resulted in an arcane language unintelligible to all but a select few academics and in research, "the significance of which moves steadily toward the vanishing point" (*Humanities in America* 9). The overall effect is a failure to address universally accessible human experience and a diminished relationship between academic humanists and the rest of society. *Relativism* in humanities programs has led to a self-destructive lack of purpose and authority. If there is no objective truth, why search for it? If one text is as good as another, why bother making distinctions? If the humanities do not offer a meaningful way of knowing the meaningful, why bother at all? The link between the humanities and patriotism, made explicit by Bennett, is developed in Cheney's charge that to challenge the traditional content and character of the humanities is to "politicize" them. *Politicization* disregards the "self-critiquing" character of Western cultural tradition. It undermines the capacity of the humanities to address the larger concerns of commonly shared humanity. In practical terms, it complicates the already difficult task of developing a core curriculum, and this task is vital to the authority (and thus the very survival) of the academic humanities. Charges of racism and sexism are not only "irrelevant" in the context of the timeless, universal truth available in the humanities, they threaten the very survival of Western cultural tradition as preserved in "the best that has been thought and said."

The persistent appeal of this approach to humanities education is apparent in a front-page article in the 23 November 1988 edition of the *Chronical of Higher Education*. The article (written by Carolyn Mooney) is an account of "the first major assembly of academics intent upon "reclaiming" the university from its "radical" captivity. Named by Mooney as two "most frequently expressed" views at the conference are

> A. Many academics have abandoned rational thought and a search for the truth, and instead teach and pursue research with the goal of advancing their own political agendas. Feminist scholars in particular were accused of such behavior.

B. Colleges and universities are caving in to demands by feminists, minority group members, and other groups that they stop teaching classic texts and the values of Western culture. While works written by women and blacks are also available . . . they should not replace the classics.

Perhaps the single most important issue addressed by this conference was the necessity of a core curriculum in the humanities. Among those supporting this view was Boston University President John Silber, who maintained that the "humanities are the essence of education," and who spoke nostalgically of nineteenth-century requirements. In terms of this study, then, Silber's nostalgia is for the unchallenged cultural authority of the traditional humanities.

Like Bennett and Cheney, the National Association of Scholars represents an educational philosophy which entails a particular interpretive position in relation to the humanities. This educational philosophy is a traditional one in the United States, and, according to its proponents, its authority went unchallenged until the 1960s. Since then, the charge goes, disintegration and chaos have reigned, and democracy itself is threatened.

However, while it may seem self-evident that this conservative philosophy translates into a particular interpretation of the humanities, this very notion would be heartily rejected by conservative thinkers themselves. Their aim is not merely to *interpret,* but to *discover and transmit* the intended meanings of classical texts. Furthermore, and consistently, the traditional canon itself is not, to the conservative philosopher, a manifestation of certain historical or cultural understandings, but rather of eternal and universal truth. This being the case, it is not only essential that the humanities should be retained at the center of general education, but that their content and character cohere with the conservative reading. This reading is not perceived as historically and linguistically contingent interpretation, but as good epistemology in a Platonist sense. The result is what one critic has labeled "educational fundamentalism" (Graff, "Teach the Conflicts").

Advocates of other educational philosophies may well agree that the humanities should be retained in or restored to a central position in the undergraduate curricula, while disagreeing not only in terms of *why* this should be the case, but also in their normative conceptions of the humanities' content and character. Importantly, however, all of the contending philosophies claim a central dedication to democracy. Thus, it is apparent that one's normative concept of democracy determines one's normative concept of humanities education and that pedagogical debates are inherently political. (This, of course, is hardly a new observation; Aristotle voiced the same argument in the *Politics,* and North American thinkers from Jefferson to Dewey have recognized "the inescapable connection between education and the character of American polity" [Cremin 85]).

Before proceeding to other pedagogical and political positions, I will discuss at some length this decade's most thoroughly developed conservative treatment of the breakdown of cultural authority which is the humanities crisis: Allan Bloom's *The Closing Of The American Mind.*

Analysis: Allan Bloom's *The Closing Of The American Mind* (Part 1)

Allan Bloom's *The Closing Of The American Mind* was published in 1987 and enjoyed remarkable success in the market place. To the surprise of even Simon and Schuster, whose first printing of the book was limited to 10,000 copies, Bloom's critique of higher education in the United States ended the year as the tenth best-seller with sales of nearly one-half million hard-cover copies. The book became the focal point of faculty seminars, radio and television talk shows, and numerous review articles in both scholarly and popular publications. Significantly, even those unsympathetic with the author's claims recognized them as something to be reckoned with. Social philosopher Stanley

Aronowitz, for example, described Bloom's text as "the first elaborated conservative educational manifesto in decades" ("New Conservative Discourse" 205), and a multitude of other scholars (over three hundred as of April 1989), offered critical analyses. Such wide readership and scholarly attention qualify *The Closing Of The American Mind* as one of the most prominent North American texts dealing with education in the 1980s, and perhaps even in the latter half of the twentieth century.

Bloom's text is divided into three parts: 1) a description of contemporary college students, 2) a critique of American nihilism and its German origins, and 3) a study of the university within the context of philosophical tradition (and the break with that tradition). The book's subtitle, *How Higher Education Has Failed Democracy and Impoverished the Souls of Today's Students,* points clearly to Bloom's thesis, but he explains in his preface that the students to which he refers are members of a certain limited group, "the kind of young persons who populate the twenty or thirty best universities . . . those who are most likely to take advantage of a liberal education and to have the greatest moral and intellectual effect on the nation" (22). Bloom's definition of democracy is not set forth so explicitly and needs to be gleaned largely by inference; the preceding quotation, however, contains a telling clue. Like Plato's ideal state, the democracy of Bloom's vision will be led, morally and intellectually, by a select, qualified few. The students whose souls are being impoverished by higher education are precisely those who will (or should) lead, and it is in this sense that democracy is being failed.

Bloom's first five chapters are devoted to delineating the character of those students who will lead the nation in the future, those who are today "materially and spiritually free" enough to enjoy a liberal education at a top university. But despite his subtitle, Bloom indicates that the souls of such students are diminished long before they reach college. Most importantly, they arrive already thoroughly convinced that truth is relative, and they perceive this relativity as a moral postulate, the essential condition of equality.

Higher education reinforces this unfortunate outlook and thereby fails to keep faith with the founding principles of democracy, the dedication to natural rights and to the rational quest for the good life. Bloom believes that these principles were once basic to higher education. Now, however, "openness" is the sole virtue and intolerance the only absolute evil recognized by students and educators alike. Such moral emptiness precludes shared goals and visions of the public good, the very commonality necessary for democracy.

Supporting the notion that truth is relative, writes Bloom, are curricula which promote cultural pluralism and lend themselves to a vacuous discourse of values. Bloom insists that the point of requiring college courses in non-Western cultures is "to force students to recognize that there are other ways of thinking and that the Western ways are not better" (36). In other words, educators have abandoned the search for universal truth and now maintain that to claim superiority for one's own cultural worldview is ethnocentric and intolerant. Bloom's counter to this position is that if students were genuinely to learn about other cultures, they would find that "all of them think their way is best, and all others inferior" (36). Western thought, by virtue of its roots in Greek philosophy, is actually the exception; it is only in the West that we are willing to doubt the identification of good with our own way. Therefore, in attacking ethnocentrism, educators are actually asserting the superiority of the Western mind and the inferiority of other cultures. Tragically, however, students are not aware of this. They do not realize that Plato long ago demonstrated that "culture is a cave" and that the way to transcend culture is not by studying other caves, but rather by using reason to seek the good and to judge our own and others' lives solely by the standard of nature. Students cannot know this because they are either taught no philosophy at all or they are taught a version of philosophy corrupted by modern German thought. The latter (to which Bloom devotes a good deal of attention later in his text) leaves only cultural relativism and historicism as intellectual possibilities. It is this intellectual poverty that diminishes the souls of students and corrodes democracy from within.

Thus cut off from the roots of Western philosophical tradition and from the "superior moral significance" which that tradition once lent to the lives of Americans (Bloom, it should be noted, uses "America" and "Americans" to refer only to the United States and its citizens.), young persons are left with a spiritual void that modern culture cannot begin to fill. Sadly, however, most students do not even feel this void. "The longing for the beyond has been attenuated" (61). Part of this attenuation is attributable to the loss of interest in classic texts which would provide students with a basis for discontent with the present and an awareness of alternatives to it. The classics no longer command the interest of students because their (the classics') authority has been undermined by relativism: "nobody believes that the old books do, or even could, contain the truth" (58).

Another challenge to the authority of classic texts is feminism, which teaches that the classics are not only outdated but morally corrupt, sexist, and oppressive. This means that certain particularly "offensive" authors, "for example, Rousseau," are censored, or are included simply to illustrate the "distorting prejudices" and injustices of the past (66).

The diminished authority of classical texts in the lives of students is accompanied by a rejection or sheer ignorance of "high culture," art, theater, and music. The latter is particularly troublesome to Bloom, and he devotes an entire chapter to it. Applying Plato's notion that music encompasses that which is inimical to reason, Bloom concludes that rock music has "one appeal only, a barbaric appeal to sexual desire" (73). He points out that Tocqueville warned that the "character of democratic art" would be "intense, changing, crude and immediate," and he suggests that one glance at MTV confirms the Frenchman's judgment. "Nothing noble, sublime, profound, delicate, tasteful or even decent can find a place in such tableaux" (74). Bloom maintains that his primary concern is not with the "moral effects" of "this music," but rather with its "effect on education" (79).

(In light of Bloom's book as a whole, this is a rather curious distinction, but one that he makes nonetheless.) And its effect on education is devastating, a numbing of the imagination and of passion, so that even after young people "get over" their obsession for this medium, their lives are not restored to the point of recognizing choices other than between "quick fixes and dull calculation." The effects of "rock addiction" are similar, then, to those of drug addiction. For those who are hooked, "anything other than technical education is a dead letter" (80).

In his final chapter dealing with the character of contemporary students, Bloom analyzes modern relationships, and here again borrows from Tocqueville. The Frenchman recognized, writes Bloom, the difficulty of living without tradition, the dangers of stark individualism and atomism in a "merely changing continuum" (84). Today's students are living illustrations of Tocqueville's dictum that "in democratic societies, each citizen is habitually busy with the contemplation of a very petty object, which is himself." This self-centeredness is now intensified, Bloom maintains, by an "indifference to the past and a loss of a national view of the future" (86).

The decline of the family (related to feminism) and an increase in mobility are indicative of the breakdown of meaningful social attachments. With no binding past and a completely open future, "the souls of young people are in a condition like that of the first men in a state of nature—spiritually unclad, unconnected, isolated, with no inherited or unconditional connection with anything or anyone" (87). Not surprisingly, then, students feel no civic responsibility, recognize no political duty. As opposed to a time when a minority of young people inherited the responsibility of public service and understood their education as preparation for it, today almost no students expect to lead political lives or perceive even a remote connection between education and civic virtue.

In what may be his book's most controversial section, Bloom continues his discussion of modern relationships through a depiction of the association between black and white students, and the harmful effects of affirmative action programs on that association. He argues that despite the formal integration of universities, there is no genuine inter-action between Afro-American and other students. While white students "have been willing . . . to talk themselves into accepting affirmative action" and are "used to propa-ganda and the imposition of new moralities," they are not really convinced of the validity of "preferential treatment of blacks" (92). White students "suppress" their real feelings, and black students—angry that whites are "in a position to do them favors"—experience shame and resentment. The consequence is that black and white students are more sep-arated than ever. The gulf is one of hypocrisy and underlying contempt because both black and white students know that affirmative action is a sham.

Meanwhile, a "little black empire" has developed and retains its legitimacy as a result of the "alleged racism" which still prevails. Bloom's judgment is that racial dis-crimination is "ancient history" and the "black domain" con-tinues to thrive largely because affirmative action "institu-tionalizes the worst aspects of separatism" (96). His history of the Afro-American movement on university campuses proceeds as follows: In the sixties, the claim was advanced that "black students [were] second-class not because they [were] academically poor, but because they [were] forced to imitate white culture" (94). The Black Power movement, supported by "relativism and Marxism," insisted on black studies programs. Once black students became aware that they had some power in determining "what an education is," they demanded more and more "conciliatory arrangements" which have progressively undermined the integrity of the university.

"Reason," insists Bloom, "cannot accommodate the claims of any kind of power whatever, and democratic soci-ety cannot accept any principle of achievement other than merit" (96). The refusal of blacks to melt into the larger society and to honor the "ideal of common humanity" sets them at odds with even "their own noblest claims and tradi-tions in this country." Rather than accepting the knowledge

available "to man as man," they claim the right to live and
study the black experience. But Bloom maintains that black
studies programs have failed because "what was serious in
them did not interest students." In reality, he argues, blacks
"partake in the common culture with the same goals and
tastes as everyone else," but "they continue to have inward
sentiments of separateness caused by exclusion when it no
longer effectively exists" (93).

Even after black studies programs were abandoned,
however, the "black domain" reinforced by affirmative action
remains. The net result is a university without integrity, a
university which "copped-out" in the 1960s and has still not
recovered. Meanwhile, separatism has been institutionalized by policies which are despised equally by blacks and
whites and which are the source of a long-term deterioration
of race relations.

The theme of separation permeates the whole of part 1
in Bloom's text: separation of students from tradition, from
reason, from nature, from everything, in fact, which supports democracy. The section on race relations, described
above, is the first in a series of discussions dealing with the
separation of persons from each other. To Bloom, the search
for freedom and equality is basic to modernity and is legit-
imated by the principles on which the United States was
founded. But as with the struggle for racial liberation and
equality, such striving—if not informed by reason and
grounded in nature—can and has led to tragic social disintegration, a decay of relations among and between persons.

Bloom's sections on sex, divorce, love, and eros are variations on this theme. Traditional patterns of social relations
have disappeared and nothing certain has replaced them.
The "psychology of separateness," Bloom laments, is the "ap-
test description . . . for the state of students' souls" (117).
And obviously, "there is no common good" for those who are
separated both psychically and socially. Only a healthy acceptance of human nature and a dedication to reason can
provide the basis for common humanity and thus for democracy. When both human nature and reason are denied, as
they have been especially since the 1960s, social and moral

decay are inevitable. The next part of Bloom's book is an analysis of the corruption of philosophy and language which led to our situation.

Analysis: *The Closing Of The American Mind* (Part 2)

How did it come about that human nature and reason lost their philosophical authority in the latter half of the twentieth century? Although not articulated explicitly, this is the central question addressed by Bloom in the second part of *The Closing Of The American Mind,* and the title of this section's opening chapter, "The German Connection," provides a hint to his answer. According to Bloom, the notion of value relativism—which has undermined the entire Western philosophical enterprise—originated in modern German philosophy (particularly Nietzsche and Heidegger). The traditional philosophical endeavor from Socrates forward had been concerned with distinguishing the real from the apparent, the true from the false, the good from the evil. But as a consequence of widespread academic enthusiasm for the philosophy of Nietzsche in the midpart of this century, a new language developed.

> The new language is that of value relativism, and it constitutes a change in our view of things moral and political as great as the one which took place when Christianity replaced Greek and Roman paganism. (141)

This new language, Bloom explains, began with Nietzsche's declaration that "God is dead." Nietzsche's nihilism constitutes more than a rejection of theism; it is a denial of philosophy as well, a denial of reason itself. Without reason, only subjectivity remains, and the term "value" refers precisely to the "radical subjectivity of all belief about good and evil" (142).

> Good and evil now for the first time appeared as values, of which there have been a thousand and one, none rationally or objectively preferable to any other. (143)

Bloom maintains that the real target of Nietzsche's philosophical attack was modern democracy, but ironically, "the
latest models of democratic or egalitarian man find much
that is attractive in Nietzsche's understanding of things"
(144). Whereas Nietzsche glorified the extraordinary or superior individual who would rise above the masses and create new gods, his thought has been co-opted by the political
Left in the United States with unfortunate consequences.
Chief among them is the ideal of the "inner-directed" value-
creating individual, an ideal which is not only accessible to
all, but also required for psychological health and "authenticity." Bloom traces this co-optation of Nietzsche from Heidegger through Erich Fromm and David Riesman, and thus
into popular culture. He offers a lengthy critique of Woody
Allen's "Zelig" to underscore the point that we have "Amer-
icanized" nihilism, digested "Continental despair," and giv-
en them a peculiar "happy ending" (144–146).

But the grim realities of a world with "nothing determinate, nothing that has a referent" are radically at odds
with the philosophical tradition on which democracy depends. Our "intellectual dependency" on German thought
has brought us to a critical impasse, and it is Bloom's objective to "think through the meaning" of that dependency
and to challenge it on behalf of democracy *and* philosophy.
He maintains that he has followed with particular concern
the increasing domination of American academic and popular culture by German thought. In the 1940s, just after the
war, German philosophy "was still the preserve of earnest
intellectuals," most of whom were either German émigrés or
Americans who had studied in Germany before the Nazi era.
At the University of Chicago, for instance, work in the social
sciences was dominated by the theories of Freud and Weber,
both of whom were profoundly influenced by Nietzsche.
While it was evident that German thought had taken an
"antirational and antiliberal" turn, a blind eye was turned to
this tendency. To the contrary, the psychological and sociological theories which were developed by German thinkers
were considered "scientific," and American intellectuals believed that "scientific progress would be related to social and

political progress." (Bloom claims that "all" of his professors
at the University of Chicago "were either Marxists or New
Deal Liberals" [149].)

It is not an exceedingly rare event in history, writes
Bloom, for one nation with a powerful intellectual life to
influence profoundly a less intellectually developed nation.
The influence of Greece on Rome and that of France on
Russia and Germany are cases in point. But the influence of
Germany on the United States in this century is remarkable
for its difference from those earlier examples, and this difference is precisely what renders our situation so problematic. Unlike the Greeks or the French who appealed to the
natural relation of "man to man" and proposed the rational
search for the "good life," regardless of gender, race, or nation, modern German philosophy taught that "the mind is
essentially related to history or culture" (153).

> German thought tended not toward liberation from one's
> own culture, as did earlier thought, but toward reconsti-
> tuting the rootedness in one's own, which has been shat-
> tered by cosmopolitanism, philosophical and political.
> (153)

Ironically, then, Americans have been seduced by a system of thought which "could never be ours and had as its
starting point dislike of us and our goals" (153). Bloom maintains that the crucial question of whether the value relativism and historicism of modern German philosophy is "harmonious" with democracy is never considered by American
academics. But he insists that the notion of value creation is
obviously contradictory to democratic rationalism. The individual rights of American citizens are grounded in Nature
and Reason. Conversely, cultural "values" are simply that—
products of culture—and to endure, they must be imposed by
force. "Rational persuasion cannot make them believed, so
struggle is necessary" (201).

> Liberal democracies do not fight wars with one another
> because they see the same human nature and the same
> rights applicable to everywhere and everyone. Cultures

fight wars with one another. They must do so because
values can only be asserted or posited by overcoming others, not by reasoning with them ... Therefore, a cultural
relativist must care for culture more than truth and fight
for culture while knowing it is not true. (202)

Nietzsche, Bloom argues, was fully aware of this and
was willing to follow the implications of his philosophical
speculations to their bitter end, the will to power, which
stands in stark contrast to the dedication to truth for which
Socrates died. While "hardly anyone [in the modern West]
swallowed what Nietzsche prescribed whole," his argument
was infectious, even more so when brewed with Marxism
into a strange new concoction of left-wing politics, particularly in France and the United States. Sartre's existential
Marxism, Bloom suggests, is a prime example of the "Nietzscheanization of the Left."

Sartre ... had all those wonderful experiences of nothing-
ness, the abyss, nausea, commitment without ground—the
result of which was, almost without fail, support of the
party line. (219)

When translated into popular language and culture, the
self-created values of "commitment, caring and determination," which resulted from the "Nietzscheanization of the
Left," thoroughly pervaded American democratic life and
were responsible for the intellectual disintegration and political chaos on university campuses in the 1960s. Thus it is
that the democratic underpinnings of higher education were
"corrupted by [the] alien views" of German philosophy.
Bloom maintains that an understanding of this part of our
intellectual history is vital if we are to "provide ourselves
with real alternatives" to the intellectual, moral, and political consequences of German thought, which "broke with
and then buried the philosophical tradition" (147). But since
the 1960s, the academy has been reaping what it sowed
earlier in this century. At risk is the survival of democracy,
for those students who will provide leadership in the future

can find no moral sustenance while the great philosophical tradition remains buried under the debris of the university.

Analysis: *The Closing Of The American Mind* (Part 3)

Bloom often appeals to Tocqueville's classic *Democracy in America,* but nowhere more fully than in the opening chapter of part 3. Tocqueville's "Intellectual Life of the Americans" is, Bloom believes, "the mirror in which we can see ourselves," and he begins his own history of the university by confirming the Frenchman's understanding that democracy's "particular intellectual bent" will, if not corrected, "distort[s] the mind's vision" (246).

The danger which democracy poses to intellectual life is "enslavement to public opinion," and for Bloom, as well as for Tocqueville, the role of the university within a democracy is to counteract that danger. Fulfilling this role means "opposing the emergent, the changing and the ephemeral," maintaining "intransigently high standards," and concentrating on the "heroic" rather than on the "commonplace." In other words, the university must "compensate for what individuals lack" and "preserve what is most likely to be neglected" (253–54). This is best accomplished, Bloom maintains, by concentrating on "philosophy, theology, the literary classics and on those scientists . . . who have the most comprehensive vision . . . of . . . the order of the whole of things" (254). Universities never fulfilled this role very well, Bloom laments, but "now they have practically ceased trying" (256).

Tracing the modern university to its Enlightenment roots, Bloom proposes that today's "crisis of the university" is intrinsically related to the "crisis of liberal democracy." The Enlightenment was not only a scientific project; it was a political one as well. "The right to freedom of thought is a political right, and for it to exist, there must be a political order that accepts that right" (258). Liberal democracy, the "best of the modern regimes," is a product of the Enlightenment project; it is a regime of reason. But "a society based on reason needs those who reason best," those, who—in effect—take "the place of kings and prelates" (258).

The true intention of the Enlightenment, Bloom argues, was the freedom of "rare theoretical men to engage in rational inquiry in the small number of disciplines that treat the first principles of all things" (261). These disciplines include not only the natural sciences, but "the sciences of man, meaning a political science that discerns the nature of man and the ends of government" (261). In short, the Enlightenment project intended freedom for philosophers (at least in the classic sense of the word). Such freedom would both reform society and secure theoretical life. These two purposes were complementary, if not identical.

Although the very term Enlightenment is connected with Plato's Allegory of the Cave, there is one important difference between the two philosophical orientations. Socrates never believed that the nature of those in the cave— the *demos*—could be altered. In other words, the unwise could never become wise, even to the extent of recognizing the wisdom of the philosopher. On the other hand, Enlightenment thinkers "meant to shine the light of being in the cave and forever to dim the images on the wall." The proper relation between the philosopher and society hinges on whether or not the cave is intractable, and the Enlightenment project intended to do in deed what Socrates believed could be created only "in speech."

The university, writes Bloom, is the Enlightenment institutionalization of Socrates' way of life. "The tiny band of men who participate fully in this way of life are the soul of the university," which in turn exists to preserve the freedom of this minority. Whereas classical philosophers never would have depended on such protection or risked being confined to the university, post-Enlightenment philosophers inhabit the university exclusively. This difference is crucial and marks a harmful change in the relation of philosophy to politics.

Genuine philosophers, writes Bloom, must engage in a "gentle art of deception." This is necessary for their very survival; "there is no moral order . . . ensuring that truth will win out in the long, or the short, run" (279). Obviously, if truth cannot be expected to win out, neither can philosophy. For philosophy even to be tolerated, it must be "thought to serve powerful elements in society without actually becoming their servant" (282). This is why ancient philosophers were proponents of aristocratic politics. The wealthy, who are drawn to the beautiful and useless, are more likely to indulge philosophy as an end in itself, even if they cannot grasp its truth. But the Enlightenment project ended that traditional relationship.

Philosophy, in its classic sense, teaches "men how to die." Enlightenment science, on the other hand, promises to enhance and prolong life. When the two were merged in the modern university, philosophy began to serve society as society actually wanted to be served. The notion of education changed from the aristocratic experience of things beautiful and useless to the enlightened self-interest of democracy. Of course, genuine philosophers "had no illusions about democracy" (289). They were aware of simply substituting one kind of deception for another. As long as they were free to pursue truth in the university, they were willing to "live with" the general vulgarity of modern society.

But the Enlightenment relegated classical philosophy to the realm of culture, a demotion which radically altered the popular and even scholarly perception of its truth claims. This perception was especially dominant in Germany. For example, the objective of German Romantic thinkers was to understand Greek culture in the interest of "founding a German culture." Plato was admired for his insights, but his intellectual activity was not perceived as qualitatively different from that of Greek poets. All were "subjective creators" of Greece's superior culture. This "discovery of Greek 'culture' was contrary to Greek philosophy," and to Bloom, the upshot was the demise of reason itself.

While this demise was hastened by Nietzsche, his project was primarily to draw out and take seriously the logical consequences of German Romanticism. In so doing, he turned the Enlightenment upon itself, and precipitated the reconstitution of the German university.

Neitzsche's . . . rigorous drawing of the consequences of what German humane scholarship really believed had a stunning effect on German university life and on the German respect for reason altogether. Artists received a new license, and even philosophy began to interpret itself as a form of art. The poets won the old war between philosophy and poetry, in which Socrates had been philosophy's champion. Nietzsche's war on the university led in two directions—either to an abandonment of the university by serious men or to its reform to make it play a role in the creation of culture.

Nietzsche's philosophical heir was Heidegger, whose teachings "are the most powerful intellectual force in our times" (311–12). They are also, in Bloom's estimation, the most destructive. Following Nietzsche, Heidegger rejected Socrates, Plato, and Aristotle, who were situated by the pair of German philosophers at the root of both Christianity and modern science. This rejection marks the ultimate denial of reason by philosophy itself. With it, "the common thread of the whole tradition . . . and the *raison d'etre* of the university as we know it" was destroyed (311).

Bloom's assertion is that Heidegger's philosophy was directly and causally linked to his early support of National Socialism. This assertion is vital to Bloom's entire thesis and encapsulates his history of the university's decline within modernity.

The university began in spirit from Socrates' contemptuous and insolent distancing of himself from the Athenian people, his refusal to accept any command from them . . . and in his serious game (in the *Republic)* of trying to impose the rule of philosophers on an unwilling people without respect for their "culture." The university may have come near its death when Heidegger joined the German people—especially the youngest part of that people, which he said had already made an irreversible commitment to the future—and put philosophy at the service of German culture. If I am right in believing that Heidegger's teachings are the most powerful intellectual force in our times, then the crisis of the German university, which everyone saw, is the crisis of the university everywhere. (311–12)

For Bloom, the blight on German universities in the 1930s has not been alleviated in the years since Heidegger delivered his famous Rectoral Address. Furthermore, what happened in Germany is happening everywhere today. The essence of the crisis of the university in this century "is not social, political, psychological, or economic, but philosophic" (312). In the United States, the "dismantling" of rational inquiry came to a head in the 1960s, but the fact that American universities "are no longer in convulsions does not mean that they have regained their health" (314).

What is called "critical philosophy" (that peculiar blend of Nietzsche and Marx described earlier), caters to "democracy's most dangerous and vulgar temptations" (319). The moral authority necessarily commanded and exercised by the university in a democracy, where there is no "living class of men" comparable to aristocrats or priests, those "natural bearers of intellectual tradition," was abandoned in the sixties and has never been reclaimed. Public opinion, as personified by "the natives, in the guise of students," rules, encouraged by "critical philosophers," who continue to urge the university's "radicalization and politicization" (324). The consequence is an anarchical institution which of course cannot begin to command and exercise cultural authority and which has thus failed democracy.

Bloom's "solution" to the breakdown of authority and the impasse which faces higher education is "one that is almost universally rejected," the "good old Great Books approach" (344). Importantly, this does not mean treating classical texts as "historical products," but "trying to read them as their authors wished them to be read." The greatest obstacle to this approach is neither students nor administrators, nor anything external to the university. Rather, "it is getting [classic texts] accepted by the faculty" (345). While this is regrettable enough among professors of the natural and social sciences, it is most lamentable and inexplicable when it comes to humanists, who might be expected to be active proponents of Great Books education.

Why has Great Books education diminished in humanities programs? Bloom lists three reasons: (1) some humanities disciplines are eager to join the sciences and to transcend their own roots in the now-overcome mythic past; (2) the jealousy and narrowness of specialization results in a tendency to defend only certain recent interpretations of the classics rather than to seek vital, authentic understandings; (3) finally, there is the general debilitation of the humanities, which is both symptom and cause of our present condition.

While Bloom maintains that "it is the humanities that have suffered most as a result of the sixties," he also declares that this suffering was altogether self-induced. The most "hysterical supporters of the revolution" were in humanities departments, where "passion and commitment, as opposed to coolness, reason, and objectivity, found their home" (354). Thus the old order, wherein the place of the humanities was assured, was not destroyed by outside forces; it was overturned from within. The humanities "have gotten what they deserved, but we have unfortunately all lost" (352).

Bloom writes that this behavior on the part of many humanists "constitutes the theme" of his entire text. Today's humanist intellectuals "do not believe in themselves or what they do." Their "democratic inclinations and guilt," together with the decadent influence of modern continental philosophy, are at odds with their vocation, which by its very definition is concerned with "the always and the contemplative . . . the rare, the refined and the superior" (353). By rejecting tradition, by transforming it into the repository of elitism, sexism, and national prejudice, humanist intellectuals have succeeded only in rendering their vocations sterile and absurd. "Like it or not," Bloom declares, the humanities attain their cultural authority from the great Western philosophical tradition. Without it, they are meaningless.

Not surprisingly, Bloom's primary concern is with the discipline of philosophy itself, whose situation within modern university humanities departments "defines ... our whole problem" (377). Having been "dethroned by political and theoretical democracy," philosophy has lost its "passion or ... capacity to rule." It has succumbed to the pressures and temptations of modernity, and "probably could disappear without being much noticed." As with all of the humanities, philosophy's demise has been self-induced. The latest scene in this suicidal drama is Deconstruction, but Bloom predicts that as long as philosophy seeks to "flatter popular democratic tastes," there will be other acts equally as degenerate.

The conclusion of Bloom's text is an appeal to the few "potential knowers" to rid themselves of the albatross of history and culture. He challenges "those who seek the truth" to rise up for the "American moment in world history, the one for which we shall be forever judged" (382).

> Just as in politics the responsibility for the fate of freedom in the world has devolved upon our regime, so the fate of philosophy in the world has devolved upon our universities, and the two are related as they never have been before. (382)

What Does Allan Bloom Want?

Despite the popular appeal of Bloom's text, it is not as easily read as might be expected, or—to put it another way—its important ideas and themes are not readily gleaned. The close reading required for the type of review just completed reveals the need to reconstruct many of Bloom's arguments, to piece them together, if one would present them in the most favorable light possible. This is due partly to Bloom's tone, which often is shrill and occasionally borders annoyingly on frenzy. (His section on rock music is a case in point.) But it also has to do with what one begins to suspect may be a studied obscurity, a deliberate attempt to engage in the philosopher's "gentle art of deception." For example, Bloom's subtitle speaks of democracy, but he never

defines the term. He appears to pit democracy and philosophy against one another, but claims that he means to
defend both. He decries moral relativism, academic narrowness, and social disintegration but makes no effort to enter
into dialogue with other contemporary thinkers who are
concerned with those same themes (e.g., Robert Bellah,
Alasdair McIntyre, or Noam Chomsky). He laments that
students feel no public responsibility or political duty, but
ignores the politics of the classroom and condemns those
who "politicize" the university. He champions the authority
of both pure reason and Western cultural tradition. Meanwhile, *The Closing Of The American Mind* is praised in a
variety of popular publications, one of which (*Reader's Digest*) claims that Bloom's book provides a "decisive answer"
to the question, "What's wrong with American education?"
Small wonder, then, that at least one critic is prompted to
query, "What on earth is going on here?" (Barber, "Philosopher Despot" 61).

In one sense, however, Bloom does offer a "decisive answer" to the *Reader's Digest* question, as well as to the one
which I have posed in the heading above. What Allan Bloom
wants is Great Books education and the cultural authority
such education exercises, the absence of which is "what's
wrong" with today's colleges and universities. Bloom believes that the authority of the Great Books tradition is a
necessary counterweight to the intellectual and spiritual
decadence of modern mass culture. He maintains that the
university's responsibility in a democracy is to transmit
Truth to those few individuals who can appreciate it and
who will provide the nation's future intellectual and moral
leadership. If the Great Books are lost, he warns, democracy
is lost. More specifically, if philosophy is lost, democracy is
lost. Even more specifically, if Platonic Realism is lost, democracy is lost. In other words, for Bloom, the concept of
democracy is necessarily grounded in human nature, which
is in turn comprehensible to "those who reason best." The
Great Books hold the key to both—human nature and reason—and thus to the success of the democratic experiment.

But to accept this "decisive answer" (which certainly is not new) is to oversimplify Bloom's book, which, as mentioned earlier, has been critiqued by several notable scholars in the years since its publication. In the following chapter I will review four such critiques, those of Martha Nussbaum, Richard Rorty, Benjamin Barber, and Stanley Aronowitz. I will also include some of my own observations and responses both to Bloom and to his critics. My purpose is to locate Bloom's voice in a conversation with others who are also committed to "education for democracy." I believe that this conversation contains no "decisive answers" but does point toward questions which promise to become ever more pressing in the coming decades.

CHAPTER TWO

"What on Earth is Going on Here?"
Some Responses to Allan Bloom's
Discourse of Crisis

Martha Nussbaum

As noted in the last chapter, Bloom links the future of democracy with the moral and intellectual leadership of "those who reason best," those who know, primarily through a process of discovery, the true nature of human beings and thus the best political arrangements. The important epistemological connection here is between knowledge and discovery, as opposed to between knowledge and creation, or knowledge and interpretation. The image of Socrates as a seeker of Truth (the image that Bloom claims has informed "the substance of his being") corresponds with the image of reasoning as a process of discovery. But classical philosopher Martha Nussbaum argues that while Bloom's "official" allegiance is to Socrates and his way of knowing, he (Bloom) is actually drawn to a far more "dogmatic and religious conception of philosophy."

In her analysis of *The Closing Of The American Mind* (*The New York Review of Books*, 5 November 1987), Nussbaum supports the thesis that Bloom is decidedly non- or even anti-Socratic. Socrates, she maintains, was interested in the "needs of different souls," and demanded "ceaseless self-questioning." Bloom, on the other hand, is "dogmatically complacent" and develops a case marked by "singleness and simplicity." Bloom's prescriptive orientation sets him apart from his self-proclaimed role model. "Bloom knows that he knows; Socrates knew that he didn't" (21).

Nussbaum also points to the tension between Bloom's frequent appeals to the authority of the ancients and his insistence upon the primacy of pure reason. The implication of her argument is that in order to keep faith with the spirit of the ancients, one must constantly question their authority. For Bloom to argue for both traditional authority and pure reason, he must appeal to the letter of ancient philosophy, just as a Christian fundamentalist appeals to the letter of the Bible. But to claim unquestioning allegiance even to the authority of Socrates himself is thoroughly non-Socratic. Thus Nussbaum disputes Bloom's understanding of the very thinker he honors most.

Central to Nussbaum's critique of Bloom's reading of ancient philosophy is the issue of sexual equality in the *Republic*. Bloom suggests that Plato's Socrates demands the sacrifice of sexual modesty and then develops the social and political consequences of that sacrifice (the "absolute liberation of women") in order to illustrate the impossibility of creating a good society without taking nature into account. Such an interpretation, writes Nussbaum, is "both bizarre and not accepted by any major non-Straussian interpreter of the text, beginning with Aristotle" (23). The latter, Nussbaum argues, studied with Plato for over twenty years and took his teacher's ideas about sexual equality seriously enough to dispute them. Bloom, however, neither mentions this, nor the fact that Plato "took the radical step of teaching women in his philosophical school," a fact that Nussbaum believes sheds a telling light on the intentions of the *Republic.**

Congruent with Bloom's rejection of feminism and feminist scholarship is his condemnation of academic programs which concentrate on non-Western cultures. Here again, Nussbaum accuses Bloom of "a most unSocratic unwilling-

---

*Interestingly, Harvey Mansfield, a defender of Bloom, lambasts Nussbaum for "feminizing" the ancients "so that they repeat her views," a move which has the awkward disadvantage of forcing her to "admit that even white males can tell the truth if it is put into their mouths" (Mansfield 34).

ness to suspect one's own ignorance" and argues that his "startling" benightedness in relation to non-Western thought serves as a "cogent, though inadvertent argument for making the study of nonWestern civilization an important part of the university curriculum" (22). Thus Nussbaum challenges Bloom as both a philosopher and a scholar.

While I wish neither to defend nor dispute Nussbaum's determination to rescue Plato from Straussian interpretation, I share her vexation with Bloom's claim that "only in the Western nations, i.e., those influenced by Greek philosophy, is there some willingness to doubt the identification of the good with one's own way." In her rejection of this notion, Nussbaum points specifically to classical Indian and Chinese thought. However, my own awareness of Eastern intellectual humility has come primarily from studying the work of the Japanese scholar, Kosuke Koyama, whose books serve as an effective refutation of Bloom's argument.

A Confirmation of Nussbaum's Critique: The Work of Kosuke Koyama

A good example of Koyama's scholarship is his 1984 *Mount Fuji and Mount Sinai,* which I find helpful when teaching introductory philosophy courses. One chapter that comes readily to mind is "The Coming of Universal Civilization," which tells of the historic encounter in Japan between Eastern and Western religious thought, particularly Buddhism and Catholicism. This chapter works well for facilitating discussions regarding differences in reasoning and the problems associated with both moral absolutism and relativism. I will describe it briefly here to underscore Nussbaum's critique of Bloom's "startling ignorance" in relation to non-Western thought.

The most telling differences between Buddhism and Catholicism are illustrated in Koyama's text by excerpts from Japan's first constitution, composed by the Buddhist prince, Shotoku (574–622), and from letters written from Japan by the Jesuit missionary, Francis Xavier. Significantly, Buddhism had been introduced to Japan only thirty-six years before Shotoku was born; thus he approached the task of writing the constitution from the perspective of one whose religious and philosophical beliefs were shared by only part of the population. (Shinto and Confucianism, for example, were developed earlier.) Shotoku, then, faced the necessity of describing judicious public interaction and discourse for a pluralistic society, and importantly, two key themes are fundamental throughout the entire constitution: *wa* and *jihi,* harmony and mercy. Article 10 is typical.

> Let us cease from wrath, and refrain from angry looks. Nor let us be resentful when others differ from us. For all men have hearts, and each heart has its own leanings. Their right is our wrong, and our right is their wrong. We are not unquestionably sages, nor are they unquestionably fools. Both of us are simply ordinary men. How can anyone lay down a rule by which to distinguish right from wrong? For we are all, one with another, wise and foolish, like a ring which has no end. Therefore, although others give way to anger, let us on the contrary dread our own faults, and though we alone may be in the right, let us follow the multitude and act like them. (152)

Koyama maintains that the philosophical virtues of *wa* and *jihi* are central to the "art of Japanese government." But these values are not theological or "real" in a Platonic sense. They are not posited as absolute givens which exist apart from concrete human situations. It may, in fact, be argued that they are thoroughly pragmatic. Furthermore, the idea that all persons are both "wise and foolish," and that none has special insight into right and wrong indicates what Koyama calls an "anthropology of humility," a perspective which disqualifies Bloom's claim that all cultures—save Western—see themselves as superior. Most important for Shotoku is not the ability or need to prove intellectual or moral superiority, but rather the desire to live harmoniously and mercifully with others. (Shotoku may indeed believe that this way of life is "best," but not in a sense which is commensurable with Bloom's use of the word.)

Shotoku's injunction to "follow the multitude and act like them" for the sake of harmony is certainly problematic when it comes to ethical life from a Western perspective. It suggests an attitude which is appalling not only to Allan Bloom, but probably to most other Westerners as well (despite Bloom's claim that "openness" has become the sole Western virtue.) Shotoku's attitude is rooted in the Buddhist negation of individual selfhood (or consciousness) and a basic understanding of life as a transitory experience to be endured with patience and serenity while awaiting the emancipation which accompanies the total eradication of self.

Such an ontology was undoubtedly appalling to the early and notable Western missionary to Japan, Francis Xavier. Koyama draws from the Jesuit' correspondence to paint a picture of the man credited with bringing Christianity to Japan. Central to Xavier's message was the idea of the infinite value of the individual soul and its immortality either in heaven or hell. Xavier's God (like Bloom's Reason) was certainly not—in his own eyes—a product of his culture. Furthermore, the values of *wa* and *jihi* (as understood by Shotoku) were not high on Xavier's philosophical priority list, let alone on his social agenda. "For Xavier," Koyama explains, "the basis of his theology of mission was firm and clear." Xavier himself put it this way:

One of the things that most of all pains and torments these Japanese is, that we teach them that the prison of hell is irrevocably shut, so that there is no egress therefrom. For they grieve over the fate of their departed children, of their parents and relatives, and they often show their grief by their tears. So they ask us if there is any hope, any way to free them by prayer from that eternal misery, and I am obliged to answer that there is absolutely none. Their grief at this affects them and torments them wonderfully; they almost pine away with sorrow ... They often ask if God cannot take their fathers out of hell, and why their punishment must never have an end. We gave them a satisfactory answer, but they did not cease to grieve over the misfortune of their relatives; and I can hardly restrain my

> tears sometimes at seeing men so dear to my heart suffer
> such intense pain about a thing which is already done with
> and can never be undone. (169–70)

Xavier worries that this "painful thought" keeps the Japanese from the true religion. In the same letter, he recounts his "satisfactory answer" to their questions.

> We began by proving to them that the divine law is the
> most ancient of all. Before receiving their institutions from
> the Chinese, the Japanese knew by the teaching of nature
> that it was wicked to . . . commit the . . . sins enumerated
> in the ten commandments. . . . We showed them that rea-
> son itself teaches us to avoid evil and to do good, and that
> this is so deeply implanted in the hearts of men, that all
> have the knowledge of the divine law from nature, and
> from God the Author of nature, before they receive any
> external instruction on the subject. (170)

In other words, Xavier's "satisfactory answer" is that because nature demonstrates the laws of God and because human reason is thoroughly capable of knowing these laws, the Japanese have no excuse. Consequently, those who had the poor timing to die before Xavier arrived with the Truth revealed in Christian doctrine were eternally damned to (the Christian-conceived) hell. The Japanese, however, found it "difficult to understand" how this God could be so cruel as to leave whole generations of people ignorant of the true doctrine and also damn them to hell forever. To the mind of the "heathen" Japanese, this God had no "integrity."

When I use this chapter from Koyama's book in introductory philosophy courses, I ask students which of the two men—Shotoku or Xavier—is most "reasonable" in his approach to ethical life, as they (the students) define it. While my teaching experiences in philosophy have not been at any of the nation's "twenty or thirty best universities" (as are Bloom's), the students with whom I am familiar are nevertheless (like Bloom's) generally supportive of tolerance and "getting along." In their view, again generally, Shotoku is an admirable figure and Xavier is not. On the other hand, most students are tremendously uneasy when it comes to abandoning the idea of absolute truth. Although they disapprove of Xavier's severity and have some budding indignation when it comes to cultural imperialism, they are certainly not willing to agree fully with Shotoku that no one can "lay down a rule by which to distinguish right from wrong." In a word, the students are ambivalent. Like Delmore Schwartz's "True-Blue American," they want "both." This, I repeat, is a general description. Some students are willing to agree fully with Shotoku; others lend complete support to Xavier. The vast majority, however, (including those who are most likely to enroll for more philosophy courses) are somewhere in the middle.

Significantly, Koyama himself points to the historical "complexity" and "confusion" surrounding the issues raised in this chapter of his book.

> In both civilizations, Buddhist East and Christian West, *wa* and *jihi* have not been practiced as they should have been. It is the civilization of "no other gods" that produced the [most deadly] bombs and actually dropped them on the cities fully inhabited by human beings, [Koyama, as a young man of fifteen years, experienced the saturation bombing of Tokyo.] and it is the civilization of "any gods welcome" of Japan that engaged in one of the most brutal killings of people during the war. (158)

I digress into this discussion of Koyama's book and my classroom experience with it for various reasons. First, I believe that Koyama substantiates Nussbaum's argument that Bloom's statements regarding the intellectual and moral superiority claimed by all cultures except the West are misinformed and misleading. Second, in my experience, today's college students—despite their understanding of tolerance as a democratic virtue—are also deeply influenced by objectivist philosophical and religious traditions, and therefore are not as willing to abandon absolute truth as Bloom claims. Finally, my reading of Plato's *Republic*, Xavier's letters from Japan, and Bloom's *The Closing Of The American Mind* indicates a common lack of qualities which may be typically absent from objectivist philosophies, that is, compassion and solidarity.

Thus, while I do not fully share Nussbaum's interpretation of Plato, I endorse her conclusion that Bloom's philosophy is "not practical, alive and broadly distributed, but contemplative and quasi-religious, removed from ethical and social concerns, and the preserve of a narrow elite" (24). This description is strengthened by the similarities apparent between Xavier's orthodox Platonic Christianity and Bloom's philosophical realism. From this it follows that, despite his book's subtitle, Bloom's real anguish is not for democracy, but for his own conception of philosophy which died, as he himself laments, along with God.

Richard Rorty

Another critic of Bloom, philosopher Richard Rorty, agrees with Nussbaum that Bloom is more concerned with his own rigid conception of philosophy than with democracy (*New Republic,* 4 April 1988). Rorty suggests, in fact, that a more exact subtitle for Bloom's book would have been *How Democracy has Failed Philosophy and Made It Difficult for Students to Take Plato Seriously* (31). He also concurs that Bloom's orientation is dogmatic and prescriptive but this tendency, he asserts, is the legacy of Platonism, inherited not only by Straussians, but by Marxists and Catholics alike. Rorty has no quarrel, then, with Bloom's interpretation of Plato, but argues that Plato himself has been rendered "obsolete" by the general success of liberal democracy.

The title of Rorty's review, "That Old-Time Philosophy," and its play on the well-known gospel song, point not only to his thesis, but also to his controversial positioning of the discipline of philosophy within the postmodern academic humanities. The latter will be explored more fully in the next chapter; for now I will limit my discussion to Rorty's review of Bloom.

Rorty, who typically writes in first-person plural, identifies himself in this essay with "Deweyan historicism" and contrasts this perspective with Bloom's Straussianism. The latter orientation, Rorty maintains, "gives one a good conscience" about one's distrust of democracy. While Bloom's mentor, the German émigré political philosopher Leo Strauss, was generally "coy" and "guarded" in his own expressions of misgiving, his students have become increasingly open, and Bloom's text is "admirably frank" in this regard. Bloom's declaration that philosophers have "always" engaged in the "gentle art of deception" points nicely to the irony of writing a book which claims to defend democracy while actually disparaging it.

But Bloom's real disgust, writes Rorty, is not with the masses but with those ("us") historicist intellectuals "who, following Emerson and Dewey, assume that the success of our 'democratic experiment' has made us contemporary Americans wiser than the Greeks" (28). Such notions as "timeless Truth" and "the nature of the Good," which Straussians still take seriously, are viewed as "obsolete" by Deweyan historicists, and this difference—not surprisingly—contributes to a generally "rancorous" relation between the two groups. Complicating the philosophical disagreement is the refusal of Straussians to participate in a "free and open forum in which [they] might argue Socratically with their opponents" (30). Straussians believe that without an essential agreement on first principles such dialogues are pointless exercises in sophistry, while historicists disavow the very concept of first principles, except as historical sediments. To the latter, then, the "Straussian remnant looks like another intolerant and self-obsessed sect" (30).

For Bloom, the health of the democratic university and of society in general must be measured against Platonic, that is, timeless and universal, standards. Without such "higher" standards, critical judgment is simply not possible. Deweyans, on the other hand, believe that by comparing the "detailed advantages and disadvantages" of certain existing institutions and modes of life with certain other real or imaginary alternatives, individuals and societies can ascertain which is preferable here and now. This type of judgment is not only sufficient; it is desirable from the democratic perspective, and furthermore, it marks the confines of the possible. Rorty maintains that Dewey "did not believe that there was such a thing as 'nature' to serve as the standard," but rather that humans are "self-creating beings" (31).

Interestingly, "both Platonists and Deweyans take Socrates as their hero" although, as might be expected, their understandings of the ancient philosopher are quite different. According to Rorty, for Plato, Socrates' objective was the Idea of the Good; for Dewey, Socrates epitomizes curiosity and the open-ended experimentation of the scientist. Perhaps this helps to explain why the "Deweyan historicist," Rorty, joins with Bloom in advocating Great Books education, at least for the first two undergraduate years. But while the philosophical (or educative) process endorsed by both men appears similar, it is undertaken in an altogether different spirit. For example, Rorty splits decisively with Bloom when it comes to the notion of epistemological unity and institutional consensus. The humanities department as "flea market"—an image which scandalizes Bloom—is perfectly acceptable to Rorty, "once the defects of our high schools have been made up for by a couple of years' worth of Great Books" (32).

In response to Bloom's charge that Nazism resulted from the demise of genuine philosophy (Platonic realism), Rorty counters that the character of German intellectual life in the 1930s led to fascism no more than North American intellectual life in that same decade led away from it. Philosophical disagreements "are just not that important in deciding how elections go, or how much resistance fascist takeovers encounter" (33). By the same token, the "spiritual malaise" which Bloom attributes in large part to the failure of American higher education is more accurately described as a national "unease" resulting from some unpleasant historical realities.

> For example: that this has not turned out to be the American Century, that the "American moment in world history" may have passed, that democracy may not spread around the world, that we do not know how to mitigate the

misery and hopelessness in which half of our fellow-hu-
mans (including a fifth of our fellow-citizens) live. (33)

In other words, North Americans are not suffering from
anything more "spiritual" than having some of the "naive"
hopes "on which we were raised" dashed against the rocks of
time.

From a Deweyan perspective, philosophy's task is neither to denigrate such hopes as "silly" or "elitist," nor to
inherit and transmit them unquestioningly and/or abstract-
ly. The task is to identify the most pressing practical issues
and problems of here and now and to debate them in a spirit
of progress and reform. The task is to help create more
genuinely democratic institutions rather than to mourn the
passing of "that old-time philosophy."

Benjamin Barber

Rorty's commitment to progressive democracy is shared
by political philosopher Benjamin Barber, whose critique of
The Closing Of The American Mind ("The Philosopher Despot") was published in the January 1988 edition of *Harper's*. Unlike Rorty, however, Barber's chief concern is with
Bloom's book as a social phenomenon, the mystery of its
remarkable popular reception. "Why are Americans so anx-
ious to welcome a book that claims they can't read," he
wonders, 'so willing to accept a polemic that excoriates their
literary intelligence?" (61)

> [Bloom] claims the country has deserted the university
> and blames democracy for the debacle, so the country
> adopts him as its favorite democratic educator. (61)

And what of educators themselves? Why are so many "besides themselves with admiration" for Bloom's "elitist agenda," his "assault on liberal tolerance and democratic education?"

Barber's attempt to "unravel" these mysteries is colored
by his provocative understanding of philosophy and democ-

racy. While I will not discuss his theories at length here, it
may be helpful to keep in mind that in his book *Strong
Democracy,* Barber raises the possibility that the story of
Socrates has another side, a side little publicized because
the "publicists have all been philosophers" (96). The relationship between Socrates and the *demos* is thus central for
Barber as indeed it is for Bloom as well. Furthermore—and
importantly—Barber's critique of Bloom makes neither the
distinction between Socrates and Plato that Rorty suggests
nor claims with Nussbaum that Bloom has misinterpreted
Plato. Rather, Barber identifies Socrates' quarrel with
Athens as the quarrel between philosophy and democracy, a
quarrel which is updated in Bloom's text and made more
complex by its conjunction with the uniquely modern quarrel between the humanist intellectual and both "European
decadence" and "American philistinism."

Barber sees Bloom as an ambivalent participant in the
modern quarrel. While Bloom is suspicious of European relativism and cynicism, he is even more suspicious of America's "self-righteous innocence" and anti-intellectualism.
While he is a loyal American and would protect his home-
land from the corruption of European nihilism, still he cher-
ishes Europe and disdains America's "spirited practicality."
From Bloom's belief that the United States has no intellectual life apart from that imported from Europe and his
equally strong conviction that European intellectual life is
tainted, it follows that he recognizes no option except for a
renewed appeal to the ancients.

But Barber spots a fly in Bloom's back-to-the-ancients
ointment. "As a modern, Bloom cannot really deny that the
credentials for both Absolute Truth and a Supreme Being
have become philosophically suspect" ("Despot" 63). (Of
course, it could be argued that Plato's Socrates also noticed
the same fly; hence the Noble Lie.) Thus, Barber compares
Bloom to Voltaire ("who urges gentlemen to send their ser-
vants out of the room" before debating God's existence), and
he argues that Bloom actually worries not so much about the
character of modern philosophical speculation as about what
the "barbarians" may make of it.

In other words, Bloom's real concern is that mass America—which has a "penchant for the vulgar, the novel, and the experimental"—should certainly not be exposed to such "grim tidings" as the death of God and philosophical relativism. "Because the masses are unfit for philosophy, the Truth leaves them defenseless and renders them dangerous" ("Despot" 63). Deprived of traditional moral authority, the barbarians will revolt. Barber thus paraphrases Bloom's implied message: "If God is dead, don't tell the Americans!" (64). This message illustrates Bloom's understanding of the correct relationship between philosophy and democracy. His solution to the ills of modernity is to initiate the few into the privileged domain of philosophy and to placate the many with "a diet of noble lies such as may be required to insulate the university from mediocrity and democratic taste" (64).

The grand irony is that Bloom's book has been so well received. What is to be made of such a paradox? Barber offers some engaging possibilities in answer to this question. He maintains that those who are sympathetic with Bloom are not "mere conservatives, but . . . zealots" (64). They require and demand Truth, Certainty, Comfort. This apparently means that such readers do not grasp Bloom's real, albeit implied, message as it is understood by Barber, that is, that only a select few are intellectually capable of living the philosophical life, of bearing up under the "grim tidings" of the death of God. Thus, Barber suggests that those who are persuaded by Bloom are in fact receiving his explicit, but false, message, that which offers "certainty to the confused and comfort to the fearful."

The picture painted by Barber, then, is of a book which claims to support democracy while undermining it, championed by readers who claim to cherish democracy while despising it. In this reading, Bloom appeals most to the very masses he denigrates, those who should not be allowed into the sacred halls of philosophy departments. In an ironic sense, this would square with Bloom's insistence that philosophers have "always" engaged in the "gentle art of deception," an activity necessitated by the inability of the masses to perceive or endure Truth. Those who are "deceived" by

Bloom's book need what it only pretends to offer, a return to the moral authority of those who know the Truth. Furthermore, according to Barber, the only "rival" to such deception, now as in Socrates' Athens, is democracy.

Contemporary French Philosophy and Barber's Concept of Democracy: Some Common Themes

Regardless of whether or not such deception is the intention of Bloom's book, Barber's essay presents a plausible, provocative, and disturbing explanation for the remarkable success of *The Closing Of The American Mind*. Furthermore, Barber's analysis of Bloom's text is congruous with the attacks on "totalizing reason" and "continuous history" launched by contemporary French philosophers, such as Michel Foucault and Jean-Francois Lyotard. While Bloom maintains (in his denouncement of affirmative action) that "[r]eason cannot accommodate the claims of any kind of power, and democratic society cannot accept any principle of achievement other than merit" (96), Lyotard contends, "Reason and power are the one and the same. You can dress up the first with prognosis and/or the dialectic, but you will still have the other dished up intact" (Descombes 171). Foucault's analysis of Western "continuous history," which functions as myth to "give meaning to the senseless, to rationalize the incongruous; in short, to translate the *other* into the language of the *same* (Descombes 108), is also a critical wedge into Bloom's thesis. The latter's portrayal of North American history as "the unbroken ineluctable progress of freedom and equality" with "no disputes" regarding the "essence of justice" (55), and again, "the majestic and triumphant march of the principles of freedom and equality" (97), reads almost as a caricature of the "continuous history" condemned by Foucault and the now empty "metanarratives" identified by Lyotard.

Bloom's insistence upon the radical separation of reason and power and the connection of achievement and merit is at the heart of his attack on critical philosophy which unveils reason itself as a power-laden concept. Most troubling to many critical philosophers are the ethical implications of Bloom's view. Nowhere are these implications more blatant than in his discussion of Afro-American studies. In this section, the inherent dangers associated with grounding reason exclusively in nature, thereby excluding the forces of history, become readily apparent. The chief danger of such a system is that it offers "rational" justification for racism, patriarchy, and a host of other historical evils.* This system is thus congruous with what Stephen Jay Gould calls the "scientific version" of Plato's myth of the metals, biological determinism.

In the language of Critical Theory (the critical philosophy which he detests so much), Bloom is guilty of transforming history into nature, the very action endorsed by Plato's Socrates (although not without some trepidation) in *The Republic*. The purpose of this deception is to maintain the authority of "those who know," be they philosopher-kings or any twentieth-century version thereof (including university professors).

"Those who know" in Bloom's (and Plato's) scheme are "those who reason best." In theory, such individuals rise to positions of authority by virtue of natural merit. But what is this not, in historical practice, the way things work? Is this "failure" to be charged against higher education, or more specifically—from Bloom's perspective—against the Left's appropriation and radicalization of Nietzsche, which has corrupted higher education? What exactly needs to be considered when one's object is the appropriate character of moral authority in a democracy? What if the demos come to believe that such authority does not, in practice, proceed out of the best reasoning? Is democracy really threatened by such a belief?

---

*William Bennett's notion of "moral equality," developed in his 1979 *Counting by Race* (coauthored by Terry Eastland), is another prime example of such metaphysical justification.

Stanley Aronowitz

Such questions are suggested by Rorty, Barber, and perhaps most forcefully by the final voice to be located in this conversation, Stanley Aronowitz, whose essay, "The New Conservative Discourse" (*Education and the American Dream**), was part of a 1988 symposium on education held at Indiana University of Pennsylvania. Aronowitz's essay situates Bloom's book within the conservative discourse of crisis so prevalent in the 1980s. Furthermore, Aronowitz alludes to the theories of Antonio Gramsci, whose work, I believe, is vital to any discussion of the social function of intellectuals and the issue of cultural authority.

According to Aronowitz, in the 1970s and early 1980s, "the conservative position on education reform was in sync with the revival of big business as a normative ethical institution" (203). The drive was to "technicize" education; a "back-to-basics" literacy was linked to higher productivity; computers were introduced into classrooms on a massive scale in order that students could be prepared for the workplace in the most direct way possible; and schools in general became "direct adjuncts of the corporate-driven labor market" (204–5).

A second wave of conservative reform rhetoric began during the second term of the Reagan administration. While "excellence" was still the buzzword, the emphasis shifted to a more philosophical, high-cultural attack on modernity, with the political Right portrayed as the savior of Western civilization itself, a civilization crumbling under the weight of humanism, relativism, and anti-intellectualism. While William Bennett was the "official" architect of this conservative strategy, it was Allan Bloom who provided the movement's philosophical substance in *The Closing Of The American Mind,* which Aronowitz describes as "the first elaborated conservative educational manifesto in years" (205).

---

*Excerpts reprinted by permission of Greenwood Publishing Group, Inc., Westport, CT, from *Education and the American Dream,* edited by Harvey Holtz et al. Copyright by Bergin & Garvey Publishers, Inc. © 1989.

Aronowitz's description of the content of Bloom's text is straightforward, but he recognizes and analyzes issues not addressed by other reviewers discussed here. Those who are familiar with Aronowitz's work are aware of his political sensibilities. (His earlier books include *60s Without Apology* and *Working Class Hero,* as well as the more recent *Science as Power).* Thus it is of marked importance that he begins his analysis of Bloom's book with

> . . . a sober reminder that the critique of advanced indus-
> trial societies that have identified themselves with mod-
> ernity is a powerful weapon of the Right *as much as the
> Left.* [emphasis added] (205)

Aronowitz contends, in other words, that Bloom's denunciation of liberal education practice and modern philosophy contains "all the elements of the anti-bourgeois sensibility: abhorrence for mass culture, a rejection of experience as the arbiter of both taste and pedagogy, and a sweeping attack on what is called 'cultural relativism'" (205–6). The moral chaos and decay which Bloom perceives at the heart of contemporary society are also discerned by many thinkers on the Left. In short, then, cultural criticism cuts at least two ways.

An important difference, of course, is that for Bloom "the sources [of cultural decadence and moral rot] are rarely economic and political." Certainly there is no criticism of capitalism, and Marx is scarcely mentioned, apart from the claim that he is no longer "taken seriously" by any "thinking person." As mentioned earlier, Bloom recognizes only one source of cultural decay, the corruption of philosophy, from which all historical evils flow.

While this difference is indeed crucial and should not be underestimated, and while Bloom's elitist agenda is obviously repugnant to democratic pluralists, Aronowitz maintains that there is much "common ground" between Left and Right. The commonality to which he points involves shared understandings regarding the character and social function of intellectuals. Referring specifically to another 1987 publication, *The Last Intellectuals,* by Russell Jacoby (who is

politically antagonistic to Bloom), Aronowitz declares that
the two men demonstrate similar "impulses," that is, "they
share the traditional intellectual's hostility to the twentieth
century, its cultural and social pluralism, and its loss of
tradition" (209).

As indicated above, Aronowitz's essay evokes the theories of the Italian Marxist thinker, Antonio Gramsci. Therefore, before proceeding with this discussion of Aronowitz's
review, it may be valuable to refer briefly to the ideas of
Gramsci, an acquaintance with which is helpful for fully
appreciating Aronowitz's thesis. Gramsci, a founder of the
Italian Communist Party, was imprisoned in 1926 after the
party was outlawed by the Fascists. He remained in prison
for eleven years, was released only after his health had been
destroyed, and died shortly thereafter in Rome. Most of his
philosophy is contained in letters and notebooks written
during his incarceration.

By the time of his imprisonment, Gramsci had already
decided that much of what is commonly referred to as "vulgar Marxism" (what Bloom calls the *only* Marxism) was
untenable. It was apparent that history was not driven only
by material forces, and Gramsci devoted much of his intellectual life to an analysis of cultural forms of power. His
theories are often drawn upon by contemporary left-wing
thinkers, and they bear relation to the issue of education and
moral authority. Of special import is Gramsci's idea of cultural hegemony and his work dealing with the nature and
social function of intellectuals.

Stated briefly, cultural hegemony is "the entire complex
of practical and theoretical activities with which the ruling
class not only justifies and maintains its dominance, but
manages to win the active consent of those over whom it
rules" (Gramsci 244). In this scheme, cultural institutions
such as schools, the mass media, churches, and so on, form
a "powerful system of fortresses and earthworks" which support the "sturdy structure" of civil society (238). These institutions, particularly in the West, form the ways in which
individuals think, believe, and behave, just as much, as if
not more than, material circumstances. Furthermore, many
of these institutions are the homes of intellectuals, who are

usually portrayed as free-floating and detached, "decontextualized" from issues of class, power, and politics. In schools,
for example, objectivity is viewed as not only desirable, but
necessary. "Traditional intellectuals" thoroughly embody
this apolitical role; they revel in the world of the "eternal
forms" and resist any notion that their ideas are
significantly connected to the political realities of everyday
life. On the other hand, "organic intellectuals" take the life
of the mind seriously enough to relate their ideas to the here
and now. Such intellectuals may be either conservative or
radical in political persuasion. The former provides the dominant class with moral and intellectual leadership; the latter
serves in a similar capacity for the working class. In each
class, this means appropriating the histories and experiences of the respective class served by the conservative or
radical organic intellectual for the purpose of serving the
interests of that class.

I hope that this brief digression will help to clarify Aronowitz's discussion of the similar "impulses" shared by
Bloom and many left-wing intellectuals (specifically Russell
Jacoby). Both Bloom and Jacoby perceive the proper role of
the intellectual (Bloom would say "philosopher") as counter-
cultural. But today's academic intellectual "orients students
to careers" rather than criticizing mass culture. He/She appears to have lost all authority in relation to public or political life, a fact which is deplored by both Bloom and Jacoby.
Furthermore, for both men, "the past plays a crucial part in
proposals to reconstruct a possible future" (Aronowitz, "Conservative Discourse" 209). The conservative Bloom and the
radical Jacoby join in appealing to a time "when at least a
minority was able to search for the Good and the True un-
hampered by temporal considerations such as making a living" (209). They both lament contemporary intellectual and
moral decay, and they both blame "mass culture, bureau-
cratically-wrought degraded institutions, and anti-intellectualism" for our collective woes (209).

In Gramsci's terms, then, both Bloom and Jacoby experience the organic intellectual's sense of political responsibility while at the same time appealing to the notion of an
"integrated past" in which society supported traditional in-

tellectuals. It is in the latter sense that they share "the traditional intellectual's hostility to the twentieth century." Furthermore, Aronowitz suggests that the tension between the traditional and organic impulses—or, put another way— between the timeless Truth served by traditional intellectuals and the timely political assertion and action required of organic intellectuals, "plagues all who are seriously concerned with education" (210).

Aronowitz maintains that "beyond scapegoating," Bloom's book fails to address why and how classical tradition and its gatekeepers (traditional intellectuals) lost their privileged position in the twentieth century. The notion that philosophical relativism is the chief culprit is not historically adequate, Aronowitz argues. Furthermore, it is not the case that all relativists "want to destroy the absolute spirit or eternal forms" (210). It is rather that those who appeal to the absolute and eternal have too often employed Truth as a weapon against others who have challenged existing power structures. Moreover, the "claims of high culture to humanism" find little historical legitimation.

> Every achievement of civilization—the pyramids, great works of Greek philosophy and science, the wonderful representations of the human body and soul of the Renaissance—are built on the backs of slaves, on a faraway peasantry; in short, these achievements are built on a material foundation that is nothing but the antithesis of claims of high culture to humanism. As Walter Benjamin reminds us, [forgetting this reality] is necessary to sustain "culture". . . . What the oppressed understand better than most is that intellectuals are typically servants of the mighty; they provide the legitimacy for deeds of state and private violence and exploitation, which is the meaning of the argument that every achievement of high culture is preceded by the blood of those who make it possible. (210)

While this argument indicates that the social function of the traditional intellectual is often synonymous with that of the conservative organic intellectual (insofar as both employ cultural tradition to support, implicitly or explicitly, existing power structures), Aronowitz suggests that the radical organic intellectual often faces an ambivalent relation with cultural tradition. This is witnessed not only by Jacoby's book, but most eloquently by the tension-filled debates during the early years of Bolshevik power in the Soviet Union. According to Aronowitz, in the early 1920s, members of a strong proletarian movement called for a radical break with bourgeois tradition in literature and art and for the creation of an official socialist canon—one without Tolstoy and Gogol, let alone Shakespeare and Moliere. But Lenin, Trotsky, and Bukharin all opposed this movement.

> For Lenin, the best of the bourgeois past constituted the legacy from which socialist culture would proceed. And Trotsky reminded his enthusiastic adversaries that one cannot create culture overnight or by edict. Even a short-lived movement for change cannot erase the past or produce new literary and other artistic forms. *Tradition lingers because it satisfies the human need to make sense of life, even in the midst of epochal changes.* [emphasis added] (211)

Thus, radical organic intellectuals—who stand on the opposite side of the political fence from Bloom—also appeal to cultural tradition and recognize its authority in the lives of persons. Importantly, this authority exists by virtue of "the human need to make sense of life," a universal human quality. Thus, it is apparent that the roots of "prophetic" (radical/ethical) authority are entwined in the garden of tradition with those of "priestly" or Platonic (conservative/metaphysical) authority, and one cannot bulldoze the deep soil of that garden without destroying both. This was precisely the reality recognized by Lenin, Trotsky, and Bukharin.

But today's primary issue, as Aronowitz sees it, is not political in the traditional sense just described. Rather, contemporary intellectuals, radical and conservative, face a common enemy: technocratic rationality, in terms of which *any* appeal to cultural tradition is meaningless. Despite the "reactionary content" of Bloom's text, "it reminds us of what has been lost in the drive for rationalization, of the supremacy of science over philosophy, of history over eternal essences" (211). On the other hand, intellectuals must take responsibility for the current state of affairs. Aronowitz agrees with Bloom that "philosophy after Hegel abandons the search for truth and becomes the servant of technical knowledge" (212). It is this "historical legacy" of technicization, also rooted deeply in Western philosophical tradition (Platonism itself bears some responsibility), that has turned universities into training grounds which create few spaces for genuine seekers of wisdom.

Thus, for Aronowitz, Bloom's books contains a half-truth. Anti-intellectualism is indeed rampant in American education, but the true enemy of those who desire "broadly-based, philosophically-informed scholarship and dialogue concerning burning questions of politics and culture" is not philosophical relativism or the "Neitzscheanized Left." The true enemy is the ideological hegemony of technology, the overwhelming drive to dominate all of nature—including humans—through the application of scientific techniques. It is this enemy, particularly when united with postindustrial capitalism and a form of nationalism that Bloom's philosophy appears to support, that obstructs the search for and dedication to wisdom in higher education.

Interestingly, Aronowitz's understanding coincides with a major component in the argument advanced by W. Jackson Bate, who traces the humanities crisis to late nineteenth-century Germany and the "new scientific paradigm" which originated, he believes, in that setting. (Aronowitz, however, is influenced by Critical Theory, which traces this "paradigm" to the very roots of Western philosophy.) Bate links this "paradigm" with the evil of specialization which has undermined the authority, purpose, and identity of the humanities, and although Aronowitz does not make an identical charge, his essay suggests agreement with Bate on this score. On the other hand, Aronowitz would radically disagree with Bate's contention that programs such as women's and ethnic studies are symptomatic of the humanities' decline. This is apparent in his claim that Bloom's antidemocratic call for reform aggravates rather than alleviates the ills produced by the ideological hegemony of technology. From Aronowitz's perspective, both Bate and Bloom overlook the narrow "specialization" inherent in a canon produced exclusively by white male Europeans and transmitted as "the best which has been thought and said," regardless of whether this canon is prescribed for everyone (as Bate, following Hutchins, would have it), or restricted as the legacy of an elite few (as Bloom suggests).

> For what Bloom means by reform is nothing less than an effort to make explicit what women, blacks, and working-class students have always known: the precincts of the higher learning are not for them and the educational system is meant to train a new mandarin class. Their fate is tied to technical knowledge. (212)

Thus, Bloom's exclusive agenda, his call for higher education to reproduce an elite community of scholars, his failure to recognize and feel compassion for the historical victims of Truth, and his apparent obliviousness (or even complicity) when it comes to the ideological hegemony of technology: all of these point to the unacceptability of his thesis from the perspective of Aronowitz.

On the other hand, Aronowitz warns those intellectuals "who boldly pronounce that the search for truth and the good life is not the exclusive property of the right" that if cultural tradition is to regain any significance in the lives of students, "it will have to justify itself either by its claims to pertinence or as a sociological and historical trace of the culture against which the present contends" (213).

The key issue here has to do with ways of knowing and with the character of knowledge which is perceived as most desirable. Natural and even social scientists, for example, generally do not appeal to the authority of a literary canon, because they are interested only in "knowledge that can be derived from mathematics and experiment" (214). They are primarily concerned with explanation and prediction and discourage any focus on meaning. But Aronowitz argues for an approach which entails a keen awareness of the realities of power, which necessitates "a historical perspective on the present and the future."

Aronowitz's support of historical knowledge points to tensions and ambiguities in Bloom's text (also noted by Nussbaum). On one hand, Bloom calls for an escape from the "cave" of culture and history into the sunlight of pure reason grounded in nature. On the other, he maintains that the authority of the humanities is based exclusively on tradition, and he laments its loss. While Bloom never addresses this apparent contradiction, Aronowitz makes it clear that his own philosophical orientation is dialectical. "What we know is conditioned by precedents and our social world is naturally and historically constituted" (214). Bloom's dominant tendency to transform the social and historical into the natural is thus unacceptable; but to critique this tendency is not to "dissolve everything into intersubjective relations since our relation to what is taken as nature, including our own 'nature,' is part of human formation" (214). Rather, the relation between nature and culture is historical, and is embodied in historical texts, both classical and folk/popular. In short, then, the humanities offer historical and social knowledge, but not—as Bloom would have it—objective knowledge. The historical and social knowledge available within the humanities is indeed "a part of the truth about ourselves," but a truth which needs to be "appropriated rather than revered, and with this appropriation, transformed" (215).

Such an understanding, of course, preserves precisely what Bloom abhors—the historicity of our lives and of our knowledge. It also presses the humanities into the service of human transformation, as opposed to simple transmission of cultural authority. Furthermore, it challenges the ideological hegemony of scientific knowledge because the latter is unveiled as historically and culturally situated, a "human formation." Unlike Bloom, who casts the humanities into a normative role which complements the sciences by objectively studying human nature, Aronowitz softens (if not eliminates) the contrast between the "two cultures" by showing their common embeddedness in history and culture. (In this sense, he resembles Dewey, whose insistence that science and art are of a kind as ways of knowing irked positivists and perhaps some *artistes* as well.)

A Critique of Technocratic Rationality

While Aronowitz does not address Bloom's charge that the German corruption of philosophy was causally linked to Nazism (of the four reviewers discussed here, only Rorty deals explicitly with this particular issue), it is significant that Aronowitz's critique of technocratic rationality corresponds with the analysis of many Holocaust scholars (spanning multiple disciplines) who also identify and implicate this rationality in their studies of Nazi atrocities and German complicity. For example, the origins of this intellectual orientation are explored by Frederic Lilge in his 1948 publication, *The Abuse of Learning: The Failure of the German University* (especially in chapter 3, "The Idolatry of Science"), and the role of German technocrats has been delineated by several since Lilge.* Indeed, technocratic rationality is indicted most consistently by those who engage in Holocaust studies.

The general critique of technocratic rationality goes something like this: In Nazi Germany, the well-educated corps of scientists and bureaucrats carried on "business as usual," adhering to the problem-solving methodology nurtured by their professional training (Roth and Rubenstein 231). These "technocrats" were not ideologically committed; on the contrary, they tended to view social and political issues as meaningless, having been rendered obsolete by modern science (Thomas Hughes 167). Such individuals, then, recognized only practical issues, which they approached exclusively from the perspective of technological expertise, with an eye toward cost-effectiveness and career advancement.

Many critical theorists understand technocratic rationality as an outgrowth of Enlightenment reason. Therefore, modern philosophy is perceived as partially culpable for contemporary social ills. At the same time, however, much of

---

*See, for example, Alan Berger, Thomas Hughes, Robert Jay Lifton, Franklin Littell, George Kren and Leon Rappoport, and John Roth and Richard Rubenstein.

Critical Theory is consistent with the work of Heidegger, who traces the desire to rationalize "and thus control everything on earth" to Socrates and Plato (Hollinger, "The Holocaust, Technology and Cultural Pluralism" 4). Thus, modern technological civilization is related to certain strains of ancient as well as modern philosophy, and it is this element within our intellectual heritage—this quest for certainty and control—which is problematic, not (as Bloom would have it) philosophical relativism.*

What Knowledge Is of Most Worth?
The Multiplicity of Modern Consciousness

> And I believe
> These are the days of lasers in the jungle
> Lasers in the jungle somewhere
> Staccato signals of constant information
> A loose affiliation of millionaires
> And billionaires and baby
> These are the days of miracle and wonder
> This is the long distance call
> The way the camera follows us in slo-mo
> The way we look to us all
> The way we look to a distant constellation
> That's dying in a corner of the sky
> These are the days of miracle and wonder
> And don't cry baby, don't cry
> Don't cry
>
> —Paul Simon**

---

*In religious language, this quest for certainty and control would be labeled "idolatry," which may or may not be significantly related to the fact that many (particularly Frankfurt School) philosophers who critique modern Western culture and technocratic rationality are Jewish. I believe that this connection is valid and significant—a valuable example of the power of cultural tradition even in the lives of culture critics. This is, however, obviously quite complex and ambiguous; Heidegger, for example, was certainly not Jewish and even joined the Nazi party. Leo Strauss was Jewish, but also a rabid Platonist.

**The Boy in the Bubble. Copyright © 1986 Paul Simon. Used by permission of the publisher.

Aronowitz's essay on Bloom and the conservative discourse of crisis brings vital issues to the foreground and serves as an eloquent reminder that modern cultural criticism and a profound commitment to democracy are not exclusive to political conservatives. Furthermore, those who fully support humanities education and perceive a crisis surrounding it may disagree radically on the sources and character of the crisis. While it may be true that the cultural authority of the humanities depends upon the authority of historical knowledge, it is almost a truism that Western civilization does not provide a single, unified history from which to draw. Any attempt to reduce tradition to such a single homogeneous authority (which speaks to "man as man") is antithetical to democracy, and, moreover, flies in the face of the "enormous multiplicity" of modern consciousness. As Clifford Geertz puts it:

> The hallmark of modern consciousness . . . is its enormous multiplicity. For our time and forward, the image of a general orientation, perspective, *Weltanschauung,* growing out of humanistic studies (or, for that matter, out of scientific ones) and shaping the direction of culture is a chimera. Not only is the class basis for such a unitary "humanism" completely absent, gone with a lot of other things like adequate bathtubs and comfortable taxis, but, even more important, the agreement on the foundations of scholarly authority, old books and old manners, has disappeared . . . The conception of a "new humanism," of forging some general "the best that is being thought and said" ideology and working it into the curriculum [seems] not merely implausible but utopian altogether. Possibly, indeed, a bit worrisome. (*Local Knowledge* 161)

It is this "enormous multiplicity" of consciousness that challenges our traditional notions of higher education, not only, as Geertz indicates, humanistic studies, but scientific ones as well. The question asked by Herbert Spencer over a century ago, "What knowledge is of most worth?" has been rendered increasingly complex by the immensity and diversity of modern thought, which has expanded both temporally and spatially. Questions of human meaning are addressed

by more and more voices in these "days of miracle and wonder." The world teems with stories that need to be told,
demand to be heard. In many cases, historically silent
voices—women, people of color—are being heard for the first
time. As their memories unfold and their histories are released, human consciousness expands, and history itself is
changed. How are we (humanist intellectuals of all political
persuasions) to decide which sources of modern consciousness are most vital as we approach a new century? What
criteria are we to use in making this judgment? While all of
the thinkers discussed thus far speak of "education for democracy," is there any common normative vision of what
that phrase means?

Having raised these questions, I should quickly add that
I harbor no illusions about arriving at "decisive answers" to
what promises to become an even more complex set of issues
in the decades ahead. However, if the notion of "education
for democracy" is to be anything other than an empty plat-
itude, the profound problems surrounding it deserve close
attention and thoughtful debate. A first step in this direction
is to define precisely what the problems and conflicts are.
For Bloom, the problems are philosophical, and in a sense, I
agree. Some epistemological conflict is inevitable in the
world of the late twentieth century, a world teeming with
multiple perceptions of truth and justice. But these conflicts
have not only to do with diverse ways of knowing and competing truth claims. The more immediate conflicts have to do
with structural power, that is, power over the institutions
which validate knowledge and define truth. For example,
control over the technological dissemination of information,
or over the funding of university research projects, is control
over knowledge itself. Conflicts over knowledge, then, are
not simply epistemological; they are profoundly ethical and
political.

The implications of these conflicts for democracy are
eloquently noted in Noam Chomsky's *Necessary Illusions,*
which was published in 1989. Chomsky indicates, for instance, that the "crisis of democracy" identified by the 1975
Trilateral Commission was perceived as the consequence of

"the efforts of previously marginalized sectors of the population to organize and press their demands" (2). In other words, the efforts of more and more people to articulate their own truths and to gain access to the political decision-making process threatens the notion of democracy held by many traditional thinkers. Such a notion presupposes the Platonist understanding that citizens—*for their own good*—must be exposed only to certain versions of truth and that their political participation must be limited.

Significantly, Chomsky's book was published before the Persian Gulf War, an event which underscores his thesis. During and after "Operation Desert Storm," students in my religion and philosophy classes debated the morality of the war, including the media policies dictated by the Bush Administration. Consistent with the national mood as a whole, most students were satisfied with those policies. Furthermore, they were rankled by any suggestion that their attitudes and opinions were being manipulated. But in all of my classes, a few students perceived what was happening as precisely that: thought manipulation, thought control. These students were horrified that such blatant censorship was so willingly accepted as necessary by their classmates.

In this context, many of the profound problems surrounding the notion of "education for democracy" become readily apparent. For which—for *whose*—notions of democracy are students to be educated? More specifically, what is the understanding of democracy present within the willingness of college students to condone media censorship and to accept not only their own but indeed *mass* exclusion from the political decision-making process? What is the responsibility of the humanities teacher in this particular context?

I cannot help but wonder how Allan Bloom might have answered these questions. If he published anything having to do with the character of academic life during the Persian Gulf War, I am not aware of it. But perhaps he might have been happily surprised, if my classroom experience was typical of the spring semester of 1991. The ideas of truth, freedom, and justice were debated, and Plato's *Republic* version of each seemed generally intact. With a few notable—

and for me, *redeeming*—exceptions, the Guardians were believed, their moral authority was sanctioned. They told us that "the fate of freedom in the world [had] devolved upon our regime" (Bloom 382), that we were engaged in a "holy war." And they assured us that democracy had prevailed.

CHAPTER THREE

The Crisis of the Humanities:
A Consequence of Pragmatism?

I am not a philosopher. I do not believe in reason
enough to believe in a system. What I am interested in is knowing how to behave and, more precisely, how to behave when one does not believe
either in God or in reason.

—Albert Camus

I think that philosophy is still rude and elementary; it will one day be taught by poets.

—Ralph Waldo Emerson

Introduction

In the preceding chapter, I discussed Benjamin Barber's
claim that Bloom's appeal to the ancients presupposes that
North America has no intellectual life apart from that imported from Europe and that modern European intellectual
life is tainted. One need only scan the index of *The Closing
Of The American Mind* to confirm Bloom's lack of regard for
non-European thought. Such a search quickly reveals, for
example, that he devotes more space to American enter-
tainers (Woody Allen, Michael Jackson, Benny Goodman)
than to American philosophers. Of notable absence, given
the topic of Bloom's text, is any mention of John Dewey's

classic study of democracy and education. Furthermore, while Dewey himself at least rates three references in Bloom's book, not a single reference is made to William James, George Herbert Mead, or Charles Sanders Peirce. Apparently, for Bloom, the American "home-grown" philosophical school of pragmatism is simply not worth discussing, either in terms of praise or condemnation.

In this chapter, I will present the neo-pragmatism of philosopher Richard Rorty as a significant alternative to Bloom's Platonic realism in relation to education for democracy. Central to my discussion will be the notion of moral authority as understood from Rorty's perspective.

Rorty's Revival of Pragmatism

Among these North American philosophers who have attempted to revive pragmatism in the past decade, none has been more prolific or more controversial than Richard Rorty. Since 1979, he has published three books and a multitude of essays, most of which are devoted to challenging and debunking traditional understandings of philosophy as "an ahistorical foundational discipline and tribunal of reason for the rest of culture" (Hiley 145). While Bloom laments that philosophy could fade from the modern cultural scene without anyone noticing and believes that the crisis of liberal democracy is a consequence of this diminished authority, Rorty understands foundational philosophy as a now out-worn "substitute for religion," a sort of cultural pinch hitter which itself has grown patched, shabby, and ready for retirement. Its replacement, in Rorty's scheme, is a blend of pragmatism and hermeneutics, a philosophical orientation which he believes is far more conducive to the values of liberal democracy than that "old-time philosophy." This distinction between Bloom and Rorty makes the latter's vision a significant alternative to that of the former. And, not surprisingly, the differences between the two men are reflected in their normative conceptions of education.

Although substantially influenced by the analytic tradition, Rorty's work in recent years has been largely in the areas of Continental Theory—especially Nietzsche, Heidegger, and Foucault—and American pragmatism, especially Dewey. Furthermore, Rorty sees these two philosophical orientations as thoroughly compatible, differing perhaps in tone and emphasis, but remarkably similar in doctrine ("Hermeneutics" 2). Both philosophical schools are vital for a world which has come of age, a world in which "traditional, Platonic, epistemologically-centered philosophy" is obsolete. What Dewey disparagingly called "the spectator theory of knowledge," the theory that Truth is correspondence to Reality, and that Reason is the means of discovering Truth, is equally unacceptable to Rorty. Moreover, he maintains that the intellectual movements inspired largely by Nietzsche (loosely referred to as "hermeneutics") are of a piece with Dewey's pragmatic rejection of Platonic epistemology. Thus, Rorty weaves Continental hermeneutics and American pragmatism into an understanding of philosophy which concurs with Wilfred Sellar's definition: "an attempt to see how things, in the broadest possible sense of the term, hang together, in the broadest sense of the term" (*Consequences* xiv).

Rorty distinguishes, then, between (large-P) Philosophy, which seeks timeless truth and goodness through a universal human faculty called reason, and (small-p) philosophy, which is concerned with timely truths and situational goodness. In the latter sense, poets, historians, and literary critics "do" philosophy, just as much as professional philosophers do. In this hermeneutical-pragmatic scheme, reason is not linked with discovery—as Bloom and other objectivist philosophers would have it—but with both interpretation and creation.*

---

*Rorty's own career, it should be noted, has evolved along with his philosophy. In the early 1980s, he left Princeton's philosophy department to become Kenan Professor of Humanities at the University of Virginia. And his most recent book, *Contingency, irony, and solidarity,* contains in-depth discussions of two [small-p] philosophers, Orwell and Nabokov.

Analysis: "Hermeneutics, General Studies, and Teaching"

Rorty's most direct discussion of the implications of his philosophy for education is his 1982 essay, "Hermeneutics, General Studies, and Teaching" (*Synergos Seminars,* Fall 1982). Appealing to Dewey's pragmatism and Hans-Georg Gadamer's hermeneutics, Rorty maintains that "what both men put in the place of Reason—the Platonic organ for detecting Truth—is a sense of tradition, of community, of human solidarity" (2–3). This sense, then, is what education, at its best, instills in students. Furthermore, while there may be dangers associated with "inculcating anti-Platonic views" in young persons, the sense of tradition and solidarity is an adequate defense against what is usually feared most of all, value relativism.

The similarities between Dewey and Gadamer are apparent, Rorty claims, in their commonly held understanding that experience is essentially linguistic and historical. Both men believed that the goal of inquiry and indeed of life itself is not "getting in touch with something which exists independently of ourselves," regardless of whether that something is perceived as Truth, God, or Reality. Rather, the goal is *Bildung,* self-formation, which is synonymous with Dewey's concept of growth. In this scheme, language is not a medium for expressing pre- or nonlinguistic reality (as Plato and Locke would have it). To make sense of such a notion, one would have to "get outside" of language and then examine reality in order to see if the two "match." But, first, one would have to determine what the "match" would "amount to," and neither Dewey nor Gadamer acknowledges the possibility of this determination (4).

To say that experience is essentially linguistic, Rorty maintains, is to concur with Wittgenstein that language cannot be escaped and that truth is contingent upon shared linguistic practice (or "language games"). This means that within a common language the possibility of consensus exists, but outside of this consensus, there is no appeal to "truth" recognized as valid by either Dewey or Gadamer. In other words, to posit the existence of an objective reality and then define truth as correspondence to that reality is no more meaningful than to assert that "God is on our side." Unless we have some way to determine the correspondence or the "divine approval," nothing is gained by either assertion.

The controversial upshot of this approach is that certain ugly claims advanced within particular linguistic practices, such as that created by the Nazis, are "true" from the hermeneutical-pragmatic perspective. Neither Dewey nor Gadamer offers any defense against this, Rorty believes, apart from that provided by alternative language systems which oppose Nazi "truth." Neither the Nazi nor the opposing linguistic practice, however, can claim correspondence with an objective moral reality. Rather, the moral consensus possible within a shared language is all we have as "backup." As Gadamer puts it, "The validity of morals is based on tradition" (in Rorty 5). By the same token, Dewey's assertion that growth is the only moral end suggests that the goal of growth is toward "realization of the potentialities already sketched out in the language we are now using." To say more than this requires "postulating some philosophical substitute for God and some special faculty called 'Reason' which will put us in touch with this God-surrogate" (5). While Plato and his inheritors are willing to make this postulation, neither Dewey nor Gadamer recognizes such a claim as warrantable.

Related to the idea that experience is essentially linguistic is the Hegelian claim—embraced in a somewhat modified form by both Dewey and Gadamer—that existence is essentially historical. Just as there is no escaping language, there is "no way out of our historical situation to an ahistorical view of our nature or situation or goal" (5). Thus, Rorty's version of pragmatism centers on the contingency of both language and history for the formulation of truth. This, of course, sets him at radical odds with Bloom, who perceives value relativism as the unavoidable consequence of such contingency, and who links the demise of both the moral authority of the philosophical tradition and democracy itself to this relativism.

Rorty acknowledges that students, too, respond to hermeneutical-pragmatic claims with the charge of relativism. This, he maintains, is because "even in this latter age," students still want to be Platonists. (This squares with my own experience as described in the previous chapter.) The objectivist philosophies and religions which have dominated Western culture render students largely unable to recognize any alternative besides the either/or of objectivity or relativism. But Rorty maintains that hermeneutical pragmatism offers a third—and superior—option.

> The difference between vulgar relativism and pragmatism is that pragmatism says the fact that a view is *ours*—*our* language's, *our* tradition's, *our* culture's, is an excellent *prima facie* reason for holding it. It is not, of course, a knock-down argument against competing views. But it does put the burden of proof on such views. It says that rationality consists in a decent respect for the opinions—or in Gadamer's deliberately shocking terms, the prejudices—of mankind. With Pierce and Habermas, it sees objectivity in terms of consensus rather than correspondence. (6)

The challenge to education, then, as Rorty sees it, is to help students break out of their "either/or" mentality. This, he believes, is precisely what Dewey spent a great deal of his life trying to accomplish, that is, ridding our culture of those "simple-minded dualisms" which exist as remnants of an outworn Platonism. This philosophical mission, Rorty maintains, is shared by Heidegger and Foucault, as well as Gadamer. The task recognized by all of these thinkers is that of creating a language—and thus a culture—in which "our finite and contingent sense of human community" would replace the authority of God and Reason. This is essential, Rorty suggests, for liberal democracy because inculcating a sense of community entails charging that community with the responsibility of "choosing its own destiny."

What type of education can contribute to such a culture and thus to democracy? Rorty believes that addressing this question means first freeing ourselves from another dual-

ism, the one which is generally perceived between hermeneutics and pragmatism themselves—or, put another way—
between Gadamer's "historicity" and Dewey's "scientific
method." This split, which is often characterized as an opposition between "two cultures," is not legitimate, according to
Rorty, who insists that one must consider the spirit in which
both humanistic education (with its Renaissance roots) and
scientific education (with its nineteenth-century roots) began. Both traditions grew out of the common need to break
through "established notions of intellectual authority" (7).
Both were created with the goal of liberation in mind. But,
importantly, in neither case should liberation be perceived
as an escape from language or history into "something different." Rather, both traditions represent "successive stages
in the attempt of the human race to solve its problems—
successive attempts to create a sense of communal purpose"
(7).

Thus, Rorty maintains that the historicism of Continental hermeneutics and the scientific method of Deweyan
pragmatism share a set of "moral virtues."

> ... willingness to accept experimental disconfirmation,
> willingness to listen to alternative theories, willingness to
> scrap an old paradigm and begin again with a new. (8)

What is rejected in both cases is the notion of Truth associated with Platonism (and Philosophy). This means, especially, that Dewey's emphasis on scientific method should
not be perceived as a drive to discover the Nature of Things,
for such a perception—in addition to being a misreading of
Dewey—is as much a "relic of Platonism" as Robert Hutchins's famous syllogism.

> Education implies teaching. Teaching implies knowledge.
> Knowledge is truth. The truth is everywhere the same.
> Hence education should be everywhere the same. (In Rorty
> 8)

Rorty's central theme is captured in his reply to Hutchins: "Truth is not everywhere the same, because language is

not everywhere the same, and . . . human existence is essentially linguistic and essentially historical" (8). In other words, there is no way of knowing, no linguistic practice, which lifts us out of history. The educational task, then, is to present both science and the humanities as attempts by human beings to solve human problems, as opposed to the Platonic understanding that one or the other offers special insight into the Nature of Things. (While it seems self-evident that Rorty's stance is more controversial in relation to the sciences, Bloom's book and its popular success indicate that a Platonist conception of the humanities is alive and well.)

For Rorty, the sense of human community upon which democracy depends is supported by neither God nor Reason. It is supported solely by a foundationless hope. And yet, while rejecting any foundations for hope, Rorty sees a sort of progress in history, progress "toward new [but never final] possibilities for humanity." It is in this spirit that he approaches the humanities, which he understands as offering "accounts of man's [sic] attempt to solve problems, to work out the potentialities of the language and activities available to them" (9). The "heroes" of the humanities are those who "invented new forms of communal life by inventing new songs, new discourses, new polities." The goal of the humanities, then, is to inspire "intellectual hero-worship," a task which Rorty claims is thoroughly compatible with nurturing a sense of community. In his scheme, an individual does not rise above one's community by appealing to something "higher." Rather, one confirms one's solidarity within community by "taking on" the problems of that community. Intellectual greatness is thus greatness at overcoming social problems, and the goal of inspiring intellectual hero worship is linked with the larger goal of helping students to see themselves "as part of the human species, as part of the adventure of the race" (11).

Borrowing from Whitehead, Rorty advances the notion of "Romance" as the educational theme into which intellectual hero worship and solidarity merge. Students, he declares, should be introduced to the "romance of learning," should be encouraged to "fall in love" with their heroes, and to experience solidarity not only with others who share the same "love affairs," but also with those who choose other "lovers." Moreover, Rorty believes that educators who advocate a core curriculum generally base their judgments not on some objective standard, but on memories of their own "love affairs" and the hope that students will enter into a romance with the same authors and heroes. From this it follows that Rorty has nothing against and in fact endorses core curricula, as long as individual faculties are allowed to develop them freely. (In practice, it should be noted, this translates into the decisions of the "most influential members" of individual faculties.) Beyond this moderate prescription, Rorty believes that little can be said about what humanities education should be.

> Because there is nothing general and philosophical to be said about love, there is nothing general and philosophical to be said about general studies. The truth about both lies in the details. (13)

What can be said, however, is something concrete about the particular community of which Rorty feels a member, the community of North American intellectuals, especially those who practice hermeneutics. Most of this community, Rorty believes, is "more skeptical about America than American thought has ever allowed itself to be." Many of his philosopher colleagues, see America as "rich, vulgar, cruel, and blind," and they appeal increasingly often to those thinkers who are radically critical of American liberal social thought. This has led, Rorty maintains, to a "new orthodoxy" which is beginning to spill over into undergraduate education with disturbing consequences. Deconstruction, for example, is taught as if it were the "true conceptual scheme which underlies all others." For Rorty, such developments fly in the face of what hermeneutics should stand for, not a new orthodoxy, but a healthy suspicion of all orthodoxy.

The danger associated with the tendency toward new methodological orthodoxy is that hermeneutics may eventually grow "as sterile as the tradition of positivistic science has become" (14). It may even contribute to a diminished, rather than an enhanced, sense of communal purpose by deteriorating into what its enemies (such as Allan Bloom) believe it to be, "an irrationalist expression of resentful despair." This is apparently why Rorty believes it necessary to temper the hermeneutical critique of culture (including liberal culture) with Deweyan pragmatism and its essential devotion to liberal democracy. If the former is taught as "just one more attempt to figure out what the problems are, an attempt no more privileged than any other," it can revitalize and deepen the Deweyan strain in American thought. If not, "hermeneutics" will be the name of a "cultural disaster." The purpose of hermeneutics, then, from Rorty's perspective, is to contribute to pragmatic liberalism, to encourage "the ability of American intellectuals to see their country as still theirs, by letting us fall back in love with the tradition which shaped us" (15).

Analysis: "Solidarity or Objectivity?"

Rorty's 1982 essay (reviewed above) offers a significant critique of the philosophical orientation manifested in Bloom's book. Indeed, Rorty's essay seems to anticipate Bloom's central argument against "openness" and relativism. While both men are concerned with community and democracy, their philosophical agendas are quite diverse. The differences between the two views—Rorty's neo-pragmatism and Bloom's Platonic realism—are framed in another and somewhat more theoretical essay by Rorty, "Solidarity or Objectivity?" published in 1985 (*Post-Analytic Philosophy*). The title of this essay points to its author's thesis: "there are two principal ways in which reflective human beings try, by placing their lives in a larger context, to give sense to those lives" (3). The first is in relation to a community, either historical or literary. The second is in relation to a "non-human reality," a reality that can be described without reference to other human beings. In the former case, an individual seeks solidarity; in the latter, the desire is for objectivity.

The dominant Western philosophical urge has been in the direction of objectivity. The idea of truth in this tradition is posited as something to be pursued for its own sake, a goal which promises to free its seeker from cultural parochialism. In this scheme, the intellectual is portrayed as someone who is in touch with the Nature of Things, and not as simply one who embraces and articulates the "opinions" of his/her community. According to Rorty, both "Socratic alienation" and "Platonic hope" are reflected in this view.

The Platonic distinctions between appearance and reality, opinion and truth, permeated Western culture and gave rise, Rorty believes, to the Enlightenment image of the intellectual as scientist. This image is the primary one inherited by modern thinkers, with the consequence that not only physical scientists but social philosophers employ objectivist rhetoric. Liberal social thought, for example, centers on social reform made possible by objective knowledge of ahistorical human nature. In this instance, the desire for community is also apparent, but the character of that community is transcendent and ultimate. It is a community based on metaphysical "givens" which eclipse diversity and particularity.

Rorty refers to those who wish to ground solidarity in objectivity as "realists." Such thinkers understand truth as correspondence to reality, from which it follows that they must construct both a metaphysics and an epistemology. The former provides a "special relation between beliefs and objects which will differentiate true from false beliefs" (5). The latter provides procedures for justifying beliefs, procedures which are perceived as not merely social, but natural. Realist epistemology, then, requires an account of natural cognitive abilities which link reason with nature.

In contrast to philosophical realists are those thinkers who pursue solidarity, but not objectivity. These thinkers, in Rorty's scheme, are "pragmatists." Because pragmatists view truth as (in William James' phrase) "what is good for us to believe," they need neither a metaphysics nor an epistemology. Pragmatists

> see the gap between truth and justification not as something to be bridged by isolating a natural and transcultural sort of rationality which can be used to criticize certain cultures and praise others, but simply as the gap between the actual good and the possible better. (5)

While realists seek solidarity through objectivity, pragmatists seek objectivity through solidarity. In other words, pragmatic objectivity is achieved through dialogue and greater intersubjective agreement. Truth, then, for the pragmatist, is a product of consensus; and the distinction between truth and opinion is simply the distinction between topics on which consensus is easily achieved and other topics on which it is not.

This being the case, pragmatists are often accused of "relativism" by realists. Rorty distinguishes among three separate views which are commonly lumped together under that epithet.

> The first is the view that every belief is as good as every other. The second is the view that "true" is an equivocal term, having as many meanings as there are procedures of justification. The third is the view that there is nothing to be said about either truth or rationality apart from descriptions of the familiar procedures of justification which a given society—*ours*—uses in one or another area of inquiry. (5–6)

The pragmatist, Rorty maintains, holds only the third of these views, which means that the realist's charge of relativism is problematic. At the crux of the issue is the fact that pragmatists have no theory of truth apart from consensus. From this it follows that the pragmatic account of truth has only an ethical base, not the epistemological and metaphysical one constructed by the realist. Realists, however, simply "cannot believe that anyone would seriously deny that truth

has an intrinsic nature," and consequently, they miscon-
strue the pragmatist's purely negative point as another positive theory (6).

The pragmatic understanding of truth as an ethical concept rather than a metaphysical or epistemological one leads
away from the notion of Reason as "a transcultural human
ability to correspond to Reality, a faculty whose possession
and use is demonstrated by obedience to explicit criteria"
(11). In this sense, pragmatism is the philosophical orientation best suited to democracy, for the central concern for
pragmatists is not how to define words such as "truth" or
"rationality," but is rather how to improve our social self-
image.

> If we could ever be moved solely by the desire for so-
> lidarity, setting aside the desire for objectivity altogether,
> then we should think of human progress as making it
> possible for human beings to do more interesting things
> and be more interesting people, not as heading towards a
> place which has somehow been prepared for humanity in
> advance. Our self-image would employ images of making
> rather than finding, the images used by the Romantics to
> praise poets, rather than the images used by the Greeks to
> praise mathematicians. (10)

The pragmatic orientation, then, lends itself to the values and habits which Rorty associates with liberal democracy: "toleration, free inquiry, and the quest for undistorted
communication" (11). While the pragmatist acknowledges
that he/she has no ahistorical or transcultural justification
for these values, it is also the case that such justification is
not perceived as necessary from the pragmatist perspective.
Rather, the sole justification required is that gained from
comparison and consensus. It is "exemplified by Winston
Churchill's defense of democracy as the worse form of government imaginable except for all the others which have
been tried so far" (11).

The fact that the pragmatist's justification for democracy is ethnocentric is readily admitted by Rorty. But ethnocentrism and relativism are not one and the same. Only by

"projecting his own habits of thought upon the pragmatist" does the realist perceive the two as synonymous. The latter, who sees the whole point of philosophical thought as detachment from one's particular community, simply cannot comprehend the pragmatist's desire for attachment to one's own, and the corresponding repudiation of a "universal" standpoint.

Moreover, Rorty argues that the realist, too, is ethnocentric, "no matter how much . . . rhetoric about objectivity he produces in his study." To be ethnocentric, Rorty contends, means dividing the human race into the "people to whom one must justify one's beliefs and others." The former group is made up of those "who share enough of one's beliefs to make fruitful conversation possible." On the other hand, there are many views which simply cannot be taken seriously by "Western liberal intellectuals," pragmatic or realist in philosophical orientation. The pragmatist accepts this limitation and the need "to start from where we are." The realist, bound by the same limitation, must necessarily be ethnocentric in rejecting the views that he/she cannot justify within the framework of his/her objectivist theory of truth. Thus, at the very moment of condemning and denying ethnocentricity, the realist inevitably practices it (13).

In conjunction with the above argument, Rorty contends that it is not actually the pragmatist's relativism which disturbs realists. Rather, it is that pragmatism threatens two sorts of "metaphysical comfort" to which Western philosophical tradition is accustomed. One is the notion of natural, that is, "biologically transmitted," rights; the other is the assurance of immortality. The first comfort, Rorty claims, makes no sense unless our biological species is linked to a "non-human reality [which] gives the species moral dignity." The second comfort is related to the notion of human nature as an "inner structure" which will somehow prevail over space and time.

> [E]ven if our civilization is destroyed, even if all memory of our political or intellectual or artistic community is erased, the race is fated to recapture the values and the insights and the achievements which [are our] glory. (13)

These two aspects of the realist's comfortable metaphysics underscore the inevitable ethnocentrism "to which we are all condemned" (14). Thus, with Nietzsche, Rorty charges that "the philosophical tradition which stems from Plato is an attempt to avoid facing up to contingency, to escape time and chance" (14).

Along with this significant Western tradition, however, Rorty identifies another competing philosophical perspective which is characterized by "social faith." The roots of this latter tradition are apparent in

> Socrates' turn away from the gods, Christianity's turn from an omnipotent Creator to the man who suffered on the cross, and the Baconian turn from science as contemplation of eternal truth to science as an instrument of social progress . . . (15)

Pragmatism, in Rorty's view, is the twentieth-century inheritor of this historical Western philosophical orientation, an orientation which offers only the comfort of solidarity while also rejecting despair. It is this alternative philosophical perspective which is needed to support liberal democracy in a world come of age. Platonic realism has simply run its course. It is no longer intellectually or morally tenable, having become "as transparent a device as the postulation of deities who turn out, by a happy coincidence, to have chosen us as their people" (15).

Further, and importantly, Rorty also recommends the tradition characterized by "social faith" as a counter to "the bad side of Nietzsche," the resentment which now characterizes much of high culture. This resentment, he maintains, has led to attacks on liberal social thought as an "ideological superstructure" that "obscures the realities of our situation and represses attempts to change that situation" (16). While the objectivist justification for liberal institutions and practices has "gone sour," this does not mean that those institutions and practices are corrupt or need to be abandoned. Rorty believes that Deweyan pragmatism provides an alternative justification for liberal democracy, and he sees his own philosophical task as the revival of pragmatism in the interest of reaffirming that justification. In other words, Rorty hopes to save the Enlightenment baby from being thrown out with the objectivist bathwater.

Analysis: "The Priority of Democracy to Philosophy"

A key issue raised but not fully addressed in the two essays just reviewed is the connection between the "self-formation" which is the goal of education and the pragmatic solidarity required for democracy. In other words, while it seems clear that he sees rejection of philosophical realism as a desirable—perhaps even necessary—condition for genuinely democratic solidarity, does Rorty also mean to say that it is a sufficient condition? What precisely is the connection between the fully developed "selves" who emerge from education (in Rorty's normative scheme) and democratic community? What is the relationship between philosophy after God and Reason, and democracy after God and Reason?

In a 1988 essay, "The Priority of Democracy to Philosophy" (*The Virginia Statute for Religious Freedom: Its Evolution and Consequences in American History*), Rorty suggests answers to these questions. He begins this essay with a reference to Thomas Jefferson, who "set the tone for American liberal politics when he said, 'it does no injury for my neighbor to say that there are twenty Gods or no God'" (257). While many Enlightenment intellectuals went further than Jefferson by contending that traditional religion should be discarded completely and perhaps replaced by an "explicitly secular political faith," the early American thinker sought only to "privatize" religion. Personal beliefs, then, were viewed by Jefferson as simply that—individual expressions of meaning. Such beliefs, although perhaps essential for "individual perfection," were conceived as "irrelevant" to democratic social order. However, should those beliefs be practiced in any fashion that could not be justified to a majority of the believer's fellow citizens, they would become pertinent issues. Furthermore, at that point, in Jefferson's view, the individual conscience became subordinate to "public expediency" (257–58).

There is, of course, another dimension of the Jeffersonian compromise between private and public in addition to the politically pragmatic side described above. The other—or "absolutist"—side maintains that "a universal human faculty," conscience, supplies "all the beliefs necessary for civic virtue," and needs to be vigilantly guarded as the locus of human dignity and rights. The potential tension between the absolutist and pragmatic sides of Jefferson's legacy is resolved, Rorty maintains, in a theory of truth based on consensus. "Such a theory," he explains, "guarantees that a moral belief that cannot be justified to a mass of mankind is 'irrational,'" not really a product of its proponent's universal moral faculty, but rather a "prejudice," which does not "share in the sanctity of conscience" (257–58).

Philosophy in this century, writes Rorty, has tended to erase the "picture of the self" central to Jefferson's democratic social compromise. In other words, the notion of a universal moral faculty that is possessed equally and independently by all persons has been discredited by contemporary intellectuals working in a variety of disciplines. The effect of this philosophical development has been a break in the link between truth and consensus and, in turn, a destruction of the Jeffersonian compromise. Liberal social theory has thus been largely polarized into absolutist and pragmatic camps (the former represented, in Rorty's reading, by Ronald Dworkin; the latter, by John Dewey and John Rawls).

In addition, however, a third type of social theory—"communitarianism"—has developed. Within this theory (represented by Robert Bellah and Alasdair MacIntyre, among others), both poles of Jefferson's compromise are rejected. The upshot of this rejection is that liberal institutions and culture are viewed as entities which "either should not or cannot survive the collapse of Enlightenment philosophical justification" (258–59).

While Rorty identifies three "strands" of communitarianism, he deals primarily with only one, that which claims

> ... that political institutions "presuppose" a doctrine
> about the nature of human beings, and that such a doc-
> trine must, unlike Enlightenment rationalism, make clear
> the essentially historical character of the self. (260)

In relation to this claim, Rorty poses two questions: (1) Is
there any sense in which liberal democracy *needs* philosophical justification? (2) Does a conception of the self which—
in Charles Taylor's phrase—makes "the community consti-
tutive of the individual," comport better with liberal
democracy than does the Enlightenment conception?

Rorty argues for a thoroughly negative answer to the
first of the above questions and for a qualified positive response to the second. He contends that Dewey and Rawls
have adequately demonstrated "how liberal democracy can
get along without philosophical presuppositions," but that
"if we *want* . . . a philosophical view of the self," then Taylor's
theory is best (261). However, such a theory is not as vital as
communitarians believe; democracy can flourish without it.

Rorty's argument against the need for a philosophical
justification for democracy is similar to his case for inevitable ethnocentrism developed in "Solidarity or Objectivity."
Dewey and Rawls, he maintains, have illustrated how philosophy can be bracketed from democratic social relations,
just as Jefferson bracketed religion. Philosophy, in this context, means "disputes about the nature of human beings and
even about whether there is such a thing as human nature"
(263). For both Dewey and Rawls, no such intellectual enterprise is required as a preface to politics. What is required
is a sense of history and an awareness of social relations. As
opposed to debates over whether human beings have natural rights, democracy requires only discussions aimed at
preserving and protecting the rights already established. In
other words, the cultural authority of philosophy is simply
not needed for democratic social relations. The sole authority necessary is "successful accommodation among individuals, individuals who find themselves heir to the same historical traditions and faced with the same problems" (264).
In this scheme, philosophy is, at worst, "mumbo-jumbo,"

and, at best, "a private search for perfection." It should thus go the way of religion when the issue at stake is one of social policy. One might paraphrase Rorty's argument, then, as advocating the separation of philosophy and state.

This reading of philosophy and democracy points to a theory of the self as "a centerless web of historically conditioned beliefs and desires," as opposed to a locus of innate dignity and natural rights. But Rorty asserts that even the former theory is not necessary for democracy.

> Such a theory does not offer liberal social theory a *basis*. If one *wants* a model of the human self, then this picture of a centerless web will fill the need. But for purposes of liberal social theory, one can do without such a model. One can get along with common sense and social science, areas of discourse in which the term "the self" rarely occurs. (270)

Given this separation between theories of self and social theory, what connection remains between the role of the humanist intellectual and democracy? Rorty suggests that since philosophy should now be perceived as the social equivalent of religion, that is, "a private pursuit of perfection," then there may be as many philosophical theories of self as there are religious theories. Because such theories are "irrelevant" to democracy, the "moral identities" of individuals simply do not matter in the larger political arena. The individual, in this scheme, is free "to rig up a model of the self to suit oneself . . . one's private sense of the meaning of one's life" (271).

Having said this, however, Rorty recognizes the need to "offset the air of light-minded aestheticism" which appears to color his attitude toward traditional philosophical questions. There is, he explains, a "moral purpose" behind his argument.

> The encouragement of light-mindedness about traditional philosophical topics serves the same purpose as does the encouragement of light-mindedness about theological topics. . . . [S]uch philosophical superficiality . . . helps make

the world's inhabitants more pragmatic, more tolerant,
more liberal ... (272)

In other words, Rorty has serious reasons for prescrib-
ing philosophical play. The "disenchantment of the world" is
vital for liberal tolerance. Against the communitarian critics
of modernity, Rorty argues that should democracy fail, it
will not teach our descendants a philosophical truth. Rather,
they will simply get some hints about what to watch out for
when setting up their next social order. Perhaps they might
remember that social arrangements can be viewed as cooperative experiments, rather than as attempts to "embody
a universal and ahistorical order." This memory alone, Rorty
contends, would be worthwhile.

Analysis: *Contingency, irony, and solidarity*

The separation between private perfection and social
solidarity, between philosophy and democracy, is confirmed
by Rorty in his 1989 book, *Contingency, irony, and solidarity*. In this text, he argues again that contemporary liberal
society "already contains the institutions for its own im-
provement" and that Western social and political philosophy
needs no further conceptual development (63). Rorty points
to J. S. Mill's proposal that "governments devote themselves
to optimizing the balance between leaving people's private
lives alone and preventing suffering" as "pretty much the
last word" when it comes to philosophizing about democratic
social life (63).

In implicit contrast to Bloom, who believes that modern
society is corrupt and needs to be redeemed by a return to
the authority of ancient philosophy and "those who reason
best" (and in explicit contrast to Foucault, who also
identifies the grim aspects of modern society but sees any
appeal to the authority of reason as synonymous with an
exercise of power), Rorty asserts that the ills of modern
society can be alleviated by keeping faith with the best social
image already developed and articulated in liberal social

philosophy and manifested in modern institutions, such as the free press, public universities, and so on.

In Rorty's scheme, liberal conscience and culture are the *accidental* products of such historical developments as Christianity, Newtonian science, and Romanticism. Progress is thus identified only in retrospect, from which it follows that there is no absolute future goal toward which we move. Rather, there is only the recognition that *this* is who we are and, in terms of how we came to be, *this* is what is good. Modern society, then, is judged as either moral or immoral within the confines of shared history and language.

Importantly, Rorty understands the identity of the above "we" as grounded in poetic rather than philosophical foundations. The traditional epistemological/metaphysical problem involving the character of the relation between subject and object is one which simply needs to be abandoned. The Enlightenment concepts of universalism and rationalism need not to be updated (as thinkers such as Habermas would have it) but "dissolved" and "replaced with something else" (67). This "something else" is

> ... an increasing sense of the radical diversity of private purposes ... the radically poetic character of individual lives and ... the merely poetic foundations of the "we-consciousness" which lies behind our social institutions. (67–68)

As indicated earlier, Rorty argues that the social institutions created by the poetically grounded "us" are morally adequate. Not only are philosophical or theoretical foundations unnecessary, but attempts to establish such foundations lead generally to a political attitude which Rorty finds at best counterproductive and at worst malignant, that is, "one which will lead you to think that there is some social goal more important than [the liberal goal of] avoiding cruelty" (65). Behind such attempts lies a "yearning for autonomy" which should be reserved, in Rorty's view, for private life. Autonomy, he explains, "is not something which all human beings have within them and which society can release by ceasing to repress . . . " (65). Rather, it is something "which certain particular human beings hope to attain by self-creation, and which a few actually do" (65). Thus, the sort of autonomy sought by such thinkers as Nietzsche, Sartre, and Foucault could never be embodied in liberal social institutions. It is a private longing, a quest for personal authenticity and purity, and should be understood as such among citizens of liberal democracies.

The significant task for philosophy, then, is to distinguish between the poetic character of private life and the equally poetic, but morally binding, character of public life. This is the task undertaken by Rorty in his 1989 book. His approach entails distinguishing between two kinds of intellectuals: the ironist and the metaphysician. The former is one who recognizes the contingency of both history and language, and thus of his/her very sense of self. Such individuals live in a state of "meta-stability" (a term borrowed from Sartre), which means being "never quite able to take themselves seriously" in view of an awareness "that the terms in which they describe themselves are subject to change" (73–74). The metaphysician, on the other hand, is one who assumes the existence of "a single permanent reality . . . behind the many temporary appearances" and sees his/her intellectual endeavor as a quest for that eternal reality. The metaphysician thus takes him/herself very seriously. He/She assumes that "the presence of a term in [his/her] final vocabulary [the vocabulary in which we each tell "the story of our lives"] ensures that it refers to something which *has* a real essence" (74). In Rorty's scheme, the metaphysician is still attached to "common sense" in that he/she takes for granted that "statements formulated in [his/her] final vocabulary suffice to describe and judge the beliefs, actions, and lives of those who employ alternative final vocabularies" (74).

Rorty draws out his initial distinction between the ironist and the metaphysician through a discussion of their different attitudes toward books and academic compartmentalization. For example, whereas metaphysicians see libraries "as divided according to disciplines" which correspond to different objects of knowledge, ironists see them as divided only according to tradition. Whereas the metaphysician needs to distinguish among poets, philosophers, and scientists in order to judge the value of their knowledge claims and their moral authority, the ironist reads to discover "the writings of all the people with poetic gifts, all the original minds who had a talent for redescription," a genius for creating new metaphors and thus new forms of cultural life (76).

A similar distinction is apparent in relation to academic compartmentalization. For instance, the metaphysician understands philosophy as "an attempt to know about certain things—quite general and important things" (76). Its study entails reference to a certain canonical final vocabulary which describes "the way the world is." For the ironist, all final vocabularies, including that of Western philosophy, are "poetic achievements" (77). Thus, philosophy is a literary genre, and the skills required for it are literary in character. This understanding corresponds with the ironist's approach to books, because the term "literature" refers to "every sort of book which might conceivably have moral relevance—might conceivably alter one's sense of what is possible and important" (82). This being the case, the lines of demarcation between and among academic disciplines are, for the ironist, consequences of "accidental historical reasons, having to do with the way in which intellectuals got jobs in universities by pretending to pursue academic specialties" (81).

Rorty contends that literary criticism—the activity of playing off one final vocabulary against others—has gradually and perhaps semiconsciously assumed the cultural status claimed in the past by religion, science, and philosophy. This development "has paralleled the rise in the proportion of ironists to metaphysicians among intellectuals" (82). (In fact, he maintains that "the ironist is the typical modern intellectual" [89]). As a consequence, an increasingly wider gap exists between intellectuals and the public, because "metaphysics is woven into the public rhetoric of modern liberal societies (82). This situation, Rorty believes, has led to charges of elitism or social irresponsibility against ironist intellectuals by both serious thinkers and "know-nothings" whose orientation is toward metaphysics. Rorty is largely willing to disregard the latter group—religious fundamentalists, for example—who "are just instinctively defending their own traditional roles" (82). The former group, however, includes such thoughtful social philosophers as Jürgen Habermas, to whose polemics Rorty responds in this 1989 publication.

Rorty's answer to Habermas echoes his thesis in "The Priority of Democracy to Philosophy," reviewed above. Political freedom, not metaphysical truth, is the sole requirement for democracy. While Rorty concurs with Habermas that "undistorted communication" is vital for both freedom and truth, the former maintains that there is not much "to be said about what counts as 'undistorted' except 'the sort you get when you have democratic political institutions and the conditions for making these institutions free'" (84). This issue turns largely on one's understanding of ideology. Whereas Habermas and other liberal metaphysicians locate *Ideologiekritik* at the heart of their philosophical enterprise, Rorty argues that the word "ideology" means nothing more significant than "bad idea" (footnote 6, 84). As far as Rorty is concerned, then, the standard "bourgeois freedoms" based on "nothing more profound" than Western history are adequate for the health of liberal democracy.

In his response to Habermas, Rorty concentrates on two critiques of "liberal irony" which emanate from the German philosopher's arguments. The first is that liberal democracies need the "social glue" of a consensus about what is "universally human." In other words, the continuation of free institutions depends upon a metaphysical rhetoric which supports public life. The second is that it is at least psychologically inconsistent to be both an ironist (one who maintains the contingency of all moral positions) and a liberal (one who maintains that "cruelty is the worst thing we do"). Put another way, without metaphysics the liberal's moral position cannot be sustained.

Rorty's reply to the first critique is the assertion that, contrary to what was feared by "lots of people in the eighteenth and nineteenth centuries," the decline of religious beliefs—which is analogous to the loss of philosophical metaphysics—has not resulted in a radical deterioration in the health of liberal societies. In fact, he argues that the growing tendency to discount the possibility of "postmortem rewards" has strengthened many such societies. In place of future individual rewards, citizens of liberal democracies substitute "hopes for one's grandchildren," hopes that "life will eventually be freer, less cruel, more leisured, richer in goods and experiences . . . " (85–86). This type of social hope, Rorty maintains, is far more resilient and substantial than religious or other metaphysically inspired hope.

> If you tell someone whose life is given meaning by this [non-metaphysical] hope that philosophers are waxing ironic over real essence, the objectivity of truth, and the existence of an ahistorical human nature, you are unlikely to arouse much interest, much less do any damage. The idea that liberal societies are bound together by philosophical beliefs seems to me ludicrous. What binds societies together are common vocabularies and common hopes. The vocabularies are typically parasitic on the hopes—in the sense that the principal function of the vocabularies is to tell stories about future outcomes which compensate for present sacrifices. (86)

Pointing out that "once upon a time atheism, too, was the exclusive property of intellectuals," Rorty maintains that in the "ideal liberal society," nonintellectual citizens would pursue Deweyan "concrete alternatives and programs" rather than metaphysical quests for moral certainty. Just as today "most people" feel no need to answer the question "Are you saved?" Rorty's ideal society would have no need to answer such questions as "Why are you a liberal?" (87). This does not mean, however, that nonintellectual citizens would be ironists. Rorty "cannot imagine a culture which socialized its youth in such a way to make them con-

tinually dubious about their own process of socialization"
(87). By definition, irony is both private and reactive. There
is necessarily a contrast between the final vocabulary an
individual inherits and the one which he/she creates for
him/herself. It appears, then, that young persons would be
socialized as "commonsensical nonmetaphysicians" in
Rorty's ideal society. This means that they would be thoroughly aware of their own contingency but would feel no
doubts about it—a possibility which hinges on the prior re-
moval of all metaphysical presuppositions from public life.*

This brings Rorty to the second of the Habermasian
critiques, the charge that philosophical ironism cannot sus-
tain liberal morality even on a personal level. Here again,
Rorty's reply is reminiscent of his earlier essay.

> The idea that we all have an overriding obligation to di-
> minish cruelty, to make human beings equal in respect to
> their liability to suffering, seems to take for granted that
> there is something within human beings which deserves
> respect and protection quite independently of the lan-
> guage they speak. (88)

In other words, the liberal abhorrence for cruelty seems to
depend on a universal and ahistorical human nature, something inviolable which gives us a *reason* not to be cruel to
others. Ironism, on the other hand, rejects this justification
for moral behavior and even insists on a potentially cruel
power over others—the "power of redescription" (89).

> The redescribing ironist, by threatening one's final vo-
> cabulary, and thus one's ability to make sense of oneself in
> one's own terms ... suggests that one's self and one's

---

*The implication of Rorty's argument is that once metaphysical pre-
suppositions disappeared from society, ironism (which is necessarily
reactive) would become impossible. While Rorty does not pursue this
issue, both ironism and metaphysics would be absent from his ideal
society, and the philosophical gap between intellectuals and nonintellec-
tuals would cease to exist. A population of commonsensical liberals would
inhabit his utopia.

world are futile, obsolete, *powerless*. Redescription often
humiliates. (90)

But note, says Rorty, that redescription and humiliation are
just as much a part of metaphysics as of ironism. In fact, the
metaphysician claims to redescribe in the name of reason
itself, rather than imagination, the one claim attributed to
the ironist by Rorty. The important distinction is that the
metaphysician insists—and usually convinces his/her audi-
ence—"that they are being *educated* . . . that the Truth was
already in them and merely needed to be drawn out into the
light" (90). This, in turn, suggests that the person being
redescribed is being empowered, and when combined with
the claim that his/her previous self-description was imposed
by something oppressive within his/her culture, such empo-
werment means becoming allied with a power greater than
culture, a power such as God or Universal Truth.

   The ironist, on the other hand, offers no such assurance.
He/She cannot claim that the right redescription will free
persons from oppressive situations. Thus Rorty concludes
that the metaphysician's charge against ironism is not that
it may humiliate, but rather that it cannot empower and
shield an individual against humiliation, and does not claim
to. In fact, it is the human vulnerability to humiliation, the
sense of a commonly shared danger, which is the only "mor-
ally-relevant definition of a person" and the very ground of
solidarity for the ironist.

   To identify imaginatively with the humiliation and suffering of others and to desire the alleviation of such suffering
are the moral virtues most closely associated with the liberal
ironist. This does not mean that he/she knows a *reason* to
care about suffering, but rather that he/she hopes to notice
when it occurs to someone with whom he/she does not share
a final vocabulary. Furthermore, for the liberal ironist, the
desire to prevent or alleviate suffering is not "essentially
human." Instead, it is a response which "arose rather late in
the history of humanity . . . is still a rather local phenomenon . . . [and] is not associated with any power larger than
that embodied in . . . concrete historical situation[s]" (93).

These distinctions, Rorty maintains, are indications of why ironist philosophy is not a public philosophy; it offers no universal foundation for freedom and equality. On the other hand, ironism points to the ability of imaginative literature, defined here in the traditional narrow sense of "plays, poems, and especially novels," to contribute to solidarity by nurturing sensitivity to cruelty. Whereas the metaphysician associates philosophical theory with social hope and literature with private perfection, the ironist reverses these connections. For the ironist, "solidarity has to be constructed out of little pieces, rather than found already waiting" in a universal reality (94).

The ways in which imaginative literature nurtures sensitivity to cruelty—our own and other's—are developed concretely by Rorty in two chapters dealing with Vladimir Nabokov and George Orwell. While I will not describe his analysis in detail, it is important to note that, in both cases, he concentrates on the themes of "tendencies to cruelty inherent in searches for autonomy" and the "tension between private irony and liberal hope" (144). Rorty's objective, to overcome the dualism between the moral and the aesthetic, is a self-conscious attempt to emulate ideas posed by Dewey in *Art as Experience*. For instance, Rorty defines the "poeticized culture" of his liberal utopia as one which would concur with Dewey's assertion that

> . . . imagination is the chief instrument of the good . . . art is more moral than moralities. For the latter either are, or tend to become, consecrations of the status quo. . . . The moral prophets of humanity have always been poets even though they spoke in free verse or by parable. (in Rorty 69)

In his final chapter, "Solidarity," Rorty examines a theme which may well exist at the center of his philosophical enterprise, in that it is related to this century's greatest unsolved mystery, the Nazi Holocaust. Why, he asks, did certain European gentiles—those in Denmark or Italy, for example—demonstrate greater solidarity with the Jewish victims of Nazism than did other European gentiles, those in Belgium, for example? Were Dane and Italians somehow

more human and Belgians somehow less? Did the former
two groups identify with the plight of their Jewish neighbors
because they (Danes and Italians) possessed a "component
which is essential to a full-fledged human being" while most
Belgians lacked their component? Does this explain why
Danes and Italians manifested a greater sense of moral concern and obligation than did Belgians?

By now, of course, it is obvious that Rorty finds this
"explanation" completely unsatisfactory. Although he recognizes the inclination to seek metaphysical reasons for
historical upheavals, he urges resistance against this inclination. Rorty proposes that Danes and Italians responded
in moral fashion to the Nazi persecution of Jews for contingent historical reasons rather than for the metaphysical
ones suggested by the questions in the preceding paragraph.
In other words, Danes and Italians responded as they did
not because they perceived an abstract moral obligation to
all human beings, but because they shared with their Jewish
neighbors a common parochial identity based largely on "fellowship-inspiring descriptions" present in their final vocabularies. Furthermore, Rorty speculates that "detailed
historicosociological explanations" exist for the absence of
such "fellowship-inspiring descriptions" in the final vocabularies of most Belgians. (He does not, however, elaborate on
this speculation.)

Rorty's intention, then, is to discount the notion that
human solidarity is the abstract identification with "humanity as such." Such identification, he claims, is "a philosopher's invention, an awkward attempt to secularize the idea
of becoming one with God" (198). Insofar as solidarity exists,
it does so as a result of imaginative identification with the
suffering of others, which in turn is dependent upon historically contingent final vocabularies, poetically created conceptions of "us."

This does not mean, Rorty hastens to add, that he un-
derestimates the value of extending "our sense of 'we' to
people whom we have previously thought of as 'they'" (192).
But this value itself, he argues, is a historically contingent
one, an outgrowth of "the moral and political vocabularies"

typical of secular Western democracies. The desire for greater solidarity, then, needs to be disassociated only from its "philosophical presuppositions," not from its concrete ethical merit. Thus, in Rorty's scheme, moral progress is "indeed in the direction of greater human solidarity" (192). However, he reiterates that it is an awareness of the human vulnerability to pain and humiliation that provides the possibility for solidarity, an awareness nurtured by the "detailed descriptions of particular varieties of pain and humiliation" available in imaginative literature. Such descriptions, "rather than philosophical or religious treatises [are] the modern intellectual's principal contributions to moral progress" (192).

It is the liberal ironist who perceives both the ethical value of a reduction of human cruelty (a public good) and the radical contingency of that ethical value (a private awareness). Distinguishing between the two "makes it possible to distinguish public from private questions . . . the domain of the liberal from the domain of the ironist" (198). While the two perceptions are indeed separate, it is altogether possible—and from Rorty's perspective, desirable—for them to merge in a single person, the postmodern intellectual.

Richard Rorty: Rebel or Metamorphosed Neoconservative? (A Comparison with Camus)

Unlike most of the other thinkers discussed in this study, Richard Rorty does not often employ a rhetoric of crisis in regard to humanities education or liberal democracy. True to his depiction of the liberal ironist, Rorty appears never to take himself quite seriously. Whatever passion or sense of urgency may be his are generally veiled behind a demeanor of relaxed candor, self-assured charm, and urbane wit. His style is polished, his ideas humane, and his tone sophisticated. I find his work highly readable and intriguingly persuasive. It is also a remarkable affirmation of liberalism, particularly in the context of the 1980s, a decade in which the "L-word" became a political epithet of derision and ridicule. One suspects that chief among Rorty's projects is that of helping the political left revise its script and find its tongue in an era dominated by a conservative discourse of "values" which has pushed—or pulled—our entire political scene to far-right stage. As columnist Ellen Goodman laments:

> ...there is no unified, over-arching description of the modern liberal view: a value-system which is egalitarian, anti-war, comfortably pluralistic, and aware of the responsibilities members of a community and world have to each other. (*Des Moines Register* editorial section; 16 June 1989)

In Rorty's terms, Goodman is seeking a liberal "final vocabulary," a new self-description which is adequate to contemporary social and political challenges. Quoting from the recent work of University of Texas scholar Kathleen Jamieson, who analyzes political rhetoric, Goodman echoes the frustration of liberals with North American politics in the 1980s, a decade in which moderates such as Walter Mondale and Michael Dukakis were successfully depicted as dangerously left of mainstream and "out of touch" with "American values." Furthermore, it is important to recall that the conservative discourse of crisis discussed earlier in this study is part of the same political rhetoric. The characterization of university humanities departments as hotbeds of ethical relativism and anti-Americanism is of a piece with the conservative attempt to transform the "L-word" into an obscenity. Given this political context, Rorty's defense of "bourgeois liberalism" and the values of tolerance, free inquiry, and undistorted communication takes on particular significance.

In many ways, Rorty's views and concerns resemble those of Albert Camus, who wrote against the backdrop of another decade when liberalism was under especially severe attack, the 1950s. Both reject the consolation of transcendence and discount philosophical humanism as a basis for ethics. In Camus's terms, both thinkers face the challenge of defining the character of moral authority "when one does not believe either in God or in reason" (*Essais* 1427; qt. in Melancon 85). Both stress the dialectical value of "between" when it comes to defining truth. This value, shared by other twentieth-century thinkers such as Martin Buber and John Dewey, is apparent in Rorty's defense of truth as consensus, Camus's commitment to dialogue, and in both men's vision of solidarity as the most cherished social objective. Both identify human suffering as the sole bond among persons and point to artistic expression as the best way of sensitizing ourselves and others. Both Rorty and Camus thus confirm what Buber called the need to "imagine the real," to imagine the suffering of others so as to enter into its reality, and thus to experience compassion in the deep, rich, root sense of the word. (One major difference, of course, is that Camus's imagination extended to the writing of novels whereas Rorty remains the literary critic.)

This blurring of the distinction between the aesthetic and the moral is related to both Rorty's and Camus's resistance to what the former calls (large-P) Philosophy. Whereas the North American thinker has rankled many academic philosophers by suggesting that metaphysical language, too, is a "poetic achievement," Camus was discounted as a philosopher by those who characterized his "formulations" as "soft and insufficient" (H. Stuart Hughes 239) and his appeal to readers as emotional rather than intellectual. While Rorty, not surprisingly, employs far more philosophical jargon than does Camus, Cornel West maintains that "Rorty's style leaves the reader always enlightened and exhilarated, yet also with the quirky feeling that one has been seduced rather than persuaded . . . " (*Evasion* 197). On the other hand, Camus defined the novel as "philosophy put into images" (*Lyrical and Critical* 145). Both men, then perceive a need to rethink the form and content of philosophical inquiry.

Finally, both Rorty and Camus are critical of both Communist totalitarianism and Western greed and smugness, but neither engages in *Ideologiekritik*. Their refusal to participate in the radical project of exposing the structural de-

fects of late capitalist institutions results in the final similarity to which I will point: the two men share a common
ground when it comes to detractors. As in the case of Camus,
many of Rorty's harshest critics come from the political left.
The projects of both men have been characterized as bourgeois, individualistic, and elitist; Camus's work was branded
"reactionary," while Rorty's has been labeled "neoconservative." Such criticism dismays the North American thinker as
much as it did the Frenchman. Rorty, for example, is "aston-
ished and alarmed" to find himself "lumped" with neocon-
servatives and relieved that he "has gotten flak" from the
right, also. "Had I not," he says, "I would have begun to fear
that I had turned into a neoconservative in my sleep, like
Gregor Samsa" ("Thugs" Footnote 5, 575). Camus, unfortunately, was less cavalier; his well-publicized battle with
Sartre and others of the more radical left resulted in a case
of "writer's block" which lasted for the better part of a decade, easing only just before his death in 1960 (Lottman 1 and
601).

In the next section of this study, I will examine the
critiques of Richard Rorty issued by those who stand to his
political left and who find his views on democracy and moral
authority unconvincing, inadequate, or even pernicious.

CHAPTER FOUR

"What is the Difference that Makes a Difference Here?" Some Responses to Richard Rorty's Liberal Pragmatism

Introduction

A major issue addressed by both Rorty and Bloom is the appropriate character of the relation between the self and society in a liberal democracy. From the Platonic realist perspective of Bloom, humanities education should have as its end an awareness of and appreciation for human nature and for the eternal and universal truth that connects all human beings, truth which determines the character of the best social arrangements. The student whose reason has been educated, primarily through an acquaintance with "the best that has been thought and said," to know human nature, is the citizen who is best prepared to assume his/her place within a democracy, which itself is grounded in a natural metaphysics. Stated crudely, then, Bloom believes (1) that human nature and universal, eternal truth exists, (2) that reason is capable of knowing such truth, and (3) that contemporary humanities education, in rejecting (1) and (2), has abandoned its task of preparing future citizens. Therefore, liberal democracy itself is in grave peril.

Rorty, on the other hand, maintains that there is no human nature (apart from the sense in which humans are "naturally" cultural beings) and no such thing as timeless, universal truth. Liberal democracy has evolved largely by accident; no one planned to create liberal conscience and culture. This does not mean that democracy should not be maintained; it is the best social arrangement that we know, given who and where we are now. But its maintenance does not depend on grounding it in metaphysics, natural or otherwise. In fact, he argues that democracy needs no philosophical justification at all.

This, I believe, is why Rorty articulates no rhetoric of crisis when it comes to the humanities. Since humanities education has no immediate authoritative relation to democracy in his scheme, there is no normative concept of the humanities which needs to be defended, at least for social/ political reasons. Rorty is thus altogether comfortable in bowing to the discretion of individual faculties, charging them only with the pedagogic task of nurturing the "romance" of learning. On the other hand, in his most recent book, Rorty points to a connection between imaginative literature and "social hope" and suggests that novels and poetry, not Philosophy, can contribute most meaningfully to solidarity. Here, then, is a limited claim for the value of humanities education to liberal democracy. But this affirmation of imaginative literature is of a piece with Rorty's complete rejection of any philosophically authoritative tradition with which we might "recreate and redescribe ourselves and the world" (West, *Evasion* 203). Thus, while Rorty does not employ a rhetoric of crisis in relation to the humanities, Cornel West maintains that Rorty's work is itself "a symptom of the crisis" within the profession of academic philosophy (206–7).

Cornel West

As portrayed by West, the crisis in philosophy, and indeed for all professional humanistic scholarship, must be situated within the context of a civilization which itself is in ruins.

> Possible nuclear holocaust hovers over us. Rampant racism, persistent patriarchy, extensive class inequality, brutal state repression, subtle bureaucratic surveillance, and technological abuse of nature pervade capitalist, communist, and neocolonial countries. ("Politics" 259)

While it might be assumed that such cultural decay would command vigilant attention on the part of humanist intellectuals, particularly philosophers, such is not the case. West argues, for example, that the institution of philosophy, largely "in the grip of . . . a debilitating ethos of academic professionalization and specialization," remains unaffected by the cultural ruins which surround the academy.

> The most terrifying aspects of this [decay in North Atlantic civilization] fail to affect the discourses and practices of most American intellectuals—principally owing to unique geographical isolation, recent professional insularity, and relative economic prosperity. ("Politics" 260)

For West, this "refusal to acknowledge the urgency of the historical moment" is an "integral part of the crisis" which exists in contemporary humanistic scholarship (Introduction, *Hermeneutics* 67).

West also points to a "pervasive sense of demoralization" within academic philosophy, especially among younger faculty and graduate students. Many such individuals languish in the decline of the "Cartesian-Kantian picture of the self, world, and God," a decline that has left the "rich intellectual resources of the West . . . in disarray" ("Politics" 259). While adherents of traditional (or what Rorty calls "old-time") philosophy still wield much institutional power, they have not been able, in West's view, to revise and reform the "work of the giants" so as to breathe new life into the once vital humanistic tradition, which is now "vapid and sterile." Thus the discipline of philosophy lies "entrenched in a debased and debilitating isolation," detached from social and political concerns as well as from its own metaphysical traditions.

A similar crisis characterizes contemporary religious studies and literary criticism, indeed the humanities in general, because at its core "the current crisis takes the form of a crisis of language" (Introduction, *Hermeneutics* 67). This, West explains, is what distinguishes postmodern philosophical issues from those of modernity. Whereas modern intellectuals concentrate on self-consciousness, postmodern thinkers "reflect on the nature of the means [historical, linguistic] by which we self-consciously constitute ourselves . . . " (67). This, in turn, calls into radical question the very possibility of "self-constitution." In other words, the postmodern philosopher concentrates on the "radical finitude and sheer contingency of human existence" and on the historical and linguistic materials and practices which determine consciousness itself. This means, then, that the self-identity of postmodern humanist intellectuals is also thrown into radical question. Such individuals, whose endeavors were traditionally "wedded to the Cartesian-Kantian picture," now face their "fragile and tentative status" as cultural authorities insofar as the "quest for certainty" has itself been exposed as a transient enterprise, one which is "trapped in . . . a historical, textual, or intersubjective web from which there is no escape" ("Schleiermacher's" 82).

In many ways, West describes in fairly esoteric language the very "crisis" perceived by conservative thinkers who deplore the isolation, self-doubt, and diminished authority of academic humanists and who prescribe a return to traditional metaphysical philosophy as the only cure for the current malady. Importantly, however, West—along with Rorty—is unwilling to exchange his intellectual integrity for moral authority grounded metaphysically. As a consequence, both of them are left with a common question, phrased by West as follows:

> Given the fact that philosophy [and humanistic scholarship in general] has been wedded to the Cartesian-Kantian picture and hence the quest for certainty, does a rejection of this picture and quest entail the end of . . . philosophy and a lapse into relativism and nihilism? (Introduction, *Hermeneutics* 68)

Rorty's response to this question, discussed in the preceding chapter, is much more congenial to West than the conservative response discussed in chapter 1. However, West is far from an uncritical student of Rorty. West's approval of Rorty is on the "microinstitutional level," that is, the level of the university, particularly the philosophy department. There, Rorty's "anti-epistemological radicalism and belletristic anti-academicism are refreshing and welcome" potential antidotes for professional isolation and sterility (West, *Evasion* 207). But West argues that although Rorty "leads philosophy to the complex world of politics and culture," he "confines his engagement to transformation in the academy and apologetics for the modern West" (207). Rorty thus "demythologizes" philosophy, only to "retreat into the philosophical arena as soon as pertinent sociopolitical issues are raised" (207).

On the "macrosocietal level," the social-political-ethical level which is of primary interest to pragmatists, West challenges Rorty with the question, "[W]hat is the difference that makes a difference here?" (206). And West concludes that on this level, Rorty's philosophical project simply makes no difference.

> Rorty's neopragmatism only kicks the philosophic props from under liberal bourgeois capitalist societies; it requires no change in our cultural and political practices. (206)

In effect, then, Rorty's project for a "post-philosophical culture" is "an ideological endeavor to promote the *basic* practices of liberal bourgeois capitalist societies," a project which "seems innocuous" because of Rorty's refusal to defend such societies on metaphysical grounds (206). But for West, Rorty's "ethnocentric post-humanism" and his "historicist sense" are too nonchalantly oblivious to "the realities of power" and the "decline of liberalism" (207).

West's critique of Rorty centers on the impossibility of "historicizing" philosophy (which Rorty does) without "politicizing" it (which Rorty does not) (207). One cannot, West argues, "demythologize philosophy" without facing up to "the complex world of politics and culture." Rorty's refusal to acknowledge this aspect of his work points to its ultimate barrenness, despite its "rich possibilities."

> To undermine the privileged philosophic notions of neces-
> sity, universality, rationality, objectivity, and transcen-
> dentality without acknowledging and accenting the op-
> pressive deeds done under the ideological aegis of these
> notions is to write an intellectual and homogeneous his-
> tory, a history which fervently attacks epistemological pri-
> vilege, but remains relatively silent about forms of politi-
> cal, economic, racial, and sexual privilege. (208)

Rorty's redescription of the history of philosophy is a
delight to those "postmodern avant-gardists" with "sophisticated anti-epistemological and anti-metaphysical tastes,"
while it is the scourge of "mainstream realists and old-style
humanists." Thus, in the academy, where a "narrow but
noteworthy" battle rages for institutional authority, Rorty's
loyalty is admirably apparent. However, West argues that
Rorty's neo-pragmatism suffers from "two major shortcomings," both of which stem from its lack of "historical and
sociological perspective" and contribute to its inadequacy in
relation to larger ethical and political issues. These shortcomings are Rorty's "distrust of theory" and his "preoccupa-
tion with transient vocabularies" (209).

West critiques these shortcomings by pointing to a
"common vulgar pragmatic fallacy" which stresses consequences at the expense of analyzing specific historical practices. This fallacy is what justifies "garden variety" attacks
on pragmatism for its "crude anti-theoreticism." West maintains, however, that a "more refined pragmatism" is possible, one that continues to resist "grand theories" while
attending equally to both consequences and specific practices through an appeal to "provisional and revisable" social
theories and critiques. The goal of this more sophisticated
pragmatism is political action aimed at achieving "certain
moral consequences" (209). Furthermore, this refined pragmatism includes a focus on the mechanisms of power, including its nondiscursive forms, "such as modes of production, state apparatuses, and bureaucratic institutions."
Thus while language would still be critiqued insofar as it,
too, entails the dynamics of power, such a critique would not
be considered a self-limiting philosophical activity.

"The time is now past," West argues, "for empty academic theoreticism, professional anti-theoreticism, and complacent 'radical' anti-professionalism" (210). This means that any philosophy with purely "microinstitutional" implications is ultimately unacceptable to West, who insists that the crisis of the humanities cannot be understood if it is not placed within the context of the crisis of North Atlantic civilization itself. West thus envisions a new form of pragmatism, one which moves beyond the walls of the university and into the broader social arena, where it acts as a "moral and political weapon" against those who "rule and dominate" and for those who are "disadvantaged, degraded, and dejected" (210). He calls this approach "prophetic pragmatism," and in the following chapter, I will explore its character more fully. But first, I want to discuss several other critiques of Richard Rorty's liberal pragmatism.

Richard Bernstein

In May of 1989, following the publication of *Contingency, irony, and solidarity,* Rorty referred (in a *Chronicle of Higher Education* interview) to his next major project, a biography of John Dewey, and quipped, "[Dewey's] work is about as close as I get to a sacred text" (Winkler 8). But while Rorty has drawn heavily on Dewey in recent years, his fellow Dewey scholar, Richard Bernstein, argues that

> ... the disparity between [Rorty's pragmatism] and Dewey's primary concerns is becoming greater and greater ... for despite occasional protests to the contrary, it begins to look as if Rorty's defense of liberalism is little more than an *apologia* for the status quo—the very type of liberalism that Dewey judged to be 'irrelevant and doomed'. ("One Step Forward" 541)

Therefore, just as Martha Nussbaum disputes Allan Bloom's interpretation of his most esteemed thinker, Plato, Bernstein challenges Rorty's faithfulness to Dewey, whose philosophy Rorty most admires.

Bernstein's critique centers on Rorty's essay, "The
Priority of Democracy to Philosophy," the mood of which he
contrasts with Dewey's 1935 *Liberalism and Social Action*.Dewey's claim, as quoted by Bernstein, was that "any
liberalism which is not also radicalism is irrelevant and
doomed" (in Bernstein, "One Step Forward" 540). Furthermore, Dewey defined "radicalism" in the same text as a
"perception of the need for radical change" in "the institutional scheme of things" (540). On the other hand, according
to Bernstein, Rorty minimizes

> . . . the disparity between the 'ideals' of liberty and equ-
> ality that liberals profess, and the actual state of affairs in
> so-called liberal societies. (552)

In other words, Rorty appears to believe that liberalism is
institutionally a *fait accompli*. Hence Bernstein's charge
that Rorty's liberalism is precisely the type that Dewey characterized as "irrelevant and doomed."

Rorty's claim that the only justification needed for liberalism is the consensus of our particular historical community is also problematic for Bernstein, who, in concur-
rence with Alasdair MacIntyre, maintains that vital
traditions embody "continuities of conflict" (551). Rorty,
however, tends to assume the existence of a historical consensus that is "solid, harmonious, and coherent" (551). In
fact, Bernstein argues, Rorty substitutes a "historical myth
of the given" for the "epistemological myth of the given"
presupposed by "that old-time philosophy".

It is in this context that Bernstein points to the need to
"unpack" just what Rorty means by "we," as in "we liberals,
we pragmatists, we inheritors of European civilization"
(553–54). This unpacking reveals, Bernstein argues,
"conflicting tendencies" in Rorty's thinking. On one hand,
Rorty tends, as indicated above, to assume an "historical
myth of the given," a contention-free inherited value to
which he appeals while rejecting any possibility or even any
need to justify it philosophically. On the other hand, Rorty
demonstrates existentialist tendencies by emphasizing "our

capacity for making and self-creation" (554). In these instances, he suggests that "'we' are always free to make up
what a traditional means for us"; thus he denies, at least
implicitly, that tradition has any "determinate content"
which constrains our interpretation. In this latter sense,
Bernstein maintains that Rorty's constant references to
'we' . . . appear to be hollow—little more than a label for the
projected 'me'" (554–55).

Bernstein also critiques Rorty on grounds similar to
those used by such thinkers as Jürgen Habermas to critique
Foucault and Lyotard. The key issue here is whether or not
Rorty closes off all possibility of meaningful social criticism
and thus performs an essentially conservative function. Habermas was the first to suggest, explains Bernstein,

> . . . that the radical credentials of so-called postmodern
> and poststructuralist thinkers might be questioned, and
> that there were parallels between postmodern discourse
> and young conservative counterenlightenment dis-
> course. . . . (555)

This argument is disturbing to Bernstein as it relates to
Rorty's "defense" of "postmodern bourgeois liberalism," a
rhetoric which shares much in common with that of neocon-
servatism. Bernstein supports this criticism by pointing to
Rorty's tendency to "downplay the significance of imperial-
istic policies practiced by liberal democracies," his refusal to
question "the relation between capitalism and liberal democracy" and his "virtually unqualified endorsement to [sic]
'really existing democracy' in Western capitalist societies"
(footnote 27, 563).

These and other aspects of Rorty's philosophical project
reinforce the contrast between Dewey and Rorty with which
Bernstein begins his essay. In Dewey's terms, Rorty's liberalism is devoid of radicalism in that it perceives no "necessity of thorough-going changes in the set-up of institutions
and corresponding activity to bring the changes to pass" (in
Bernstein 540). Again, in Dewey's terms, such liberalism is
"irrelevant and doomed."

By appealing to both Dewey and Habermas, Bernstein thus charges that Rorty offers "little more than an ideological *apologia* for an old-fashioned version of cold war liberalism dressed up in fashionable 'postmodern' discourse" (556). Ultimately, then, according to Bernstein, Rorty takes "one step forward, two steps backward" (556).

Nancy Fraser

As indicated above, Bernstein attempts to "unpack"just what Rorty means by "we." Not surprisingly, several of Rorty's critics perceive a similar necessity. Furthermore, and significantly, many of the voices raised in criticism of Rorty are those which have been traditionally suppressed, or otherwise omitted from, mainstream philosophical dialogue and from political decision-making processes. Cornel West, for example, speaks out of the Afro-American experience, which he argues has "never" been "taken . . . seriously" by American philosophy (*Prophesy Deliverance* 11). In addition, at least three feminist philosophers (Rebecca Comay 1987; Dorothy Leland 1988; Nancy Fraser 1988) have offered critiques of Rorty. In this section, I will pay special attention to Fraser's essay, "Solidarity or Singularity? Richard Rorty between Romanticism and Technocracy" (*Praxis International,* October 1988).

Fraser's thesis is that Rorty's books and essays "are the site of a struggle between . . . a Romantic impulse and a pragmatic impulse" (258). Moreover, she argues that this struggle ends always in stalemate. Within its confines, Rorty "oscillates among three different views of the relationship between . . . poetry and politics," which entail three corresponding concepts of the "social role and political function of intellectuals" (258). The first view, Fraser explains, sees Romanticism (the "strong poet") and pragmatism (the "utopian reform politician") as "natural partners"; the second sees them as antithetical; the third separates them into distinct spheres, the private and public.

The Rorty who articulates the first view, which Fraser calls the "Invisible Hand" concept, links poetry with community and suggests that once the quest for objectivity is abandoned, solidarity will naturally be created. This is the Rorty who celebrates the aesthetic attitude and the romance of learning. He believes that liberal tolerance develops out of an awareness of other people's vocabularies and that such awareness is primarily erotic or imaginative in character. Fraser calls this approach a "version of the old trickle-down argument: liberty in the arts fosters equality in society" (261).

The Rorty who represents the second view, labeled by Fraser as the "Sublimity or Decency?" approach, recognizes that the creative, redescribing "ironist" may humiliate others and thus, in the eyes of the liberal, be guilty of the worst of all possible acts: cruelty. "Rorty now discerns a 'selfish,' anti-social motive in Romanticism, one that represents the very antithesis of communal identification" (262). This Rorty fears the "dark side" of Nietzsche and proposes that Deweyan pragmatic liberalism is a necessary counterweight to Romanticism in the interest of democratic solidarity. Here, then, according to Fraser, Rorty "frames the issue as Romanticism versus pragmatism": for the former, "the social world exists for the sake of the poet," whereas for the latter, "the poet exists for the sake of the social world" (263). Furthermore, this approach indicates that Rorty, whose project is to rid philosophy of objectivism, struggles between two alternatives to it: the Romantic understanding of "philosophy as metaphor" and the pragmatic understanding of "philosophy as politics" (262).

The Rorty who articulates the third view—the "Partition" position, as Fraser calls it—has "contrived a new formulation aimed at letting him have it both ways" (263). His solution is to separate Romanticism and pragmatism into two distinct spheres, the private and public. Fraser argues that Rorty's project here is to "neutralize the nonliberal political implications of radical thought" by denying that "radical thought has any political implications" (264). This is accomplished by casting radical thought into the preserve of Romanticism, the sphere of self-discovery, sublimity, and irony and keeping this sphere isolated from public life, where pragmatic social hope and solidarity merge inevitably in liberalism.

Fraser sees Rorty's "Partition" approach as "extremely interesting" and his "most sophisticated" position thus far, but she also identifies it as the most seriously flawed. This position "stands or falls," she argues, "with the possibility of drawing a sharp boundary between public or private life" (264). Moreover, it entails an image of certain humanist intellectuals as persons who must be thoroughly "domesticated, cut down to size, and made fit for private life" (264). In other words, any thinker who speaks a language nonconductive to the politics of liberalism is denied any social or political function.

From the perspective of a "whole range of New Left social movements," Fraser argues, Rorty's "Partition" position is thoroughly unacceptable. These movements, she explains, have shown that the private-public split so dear to classical liberalism is at best inadequate, and at worst, pernicious.

> Workers' movements . . . especially as clarified by Marxist theory, have taught us that the economic is political. Likewise, women's movements, as illuminated by feminist theory, have taught us that the domestic and the personal are political. Finally, a whole range of New Left social movements, as illuminated by Gramscian, Foucaultian, and yes, even by Althusserian theory, have taught us that the cultural, the medical, the educational . . . that all this, too, is political. (264–65)

Rorty's "Partition" position, Fraser maintains, requires that these insights be buried and that the last one hundred years of social history be forgotten. It does so by relegating radical theory to a "preserve where strivings for transcendence are quarantined, rendered safe, because rendered sterile" (266).

Fraser identifies two important social consequences of Rorty's "domestication" of radical theory. The first is that "there can be no legitimate cultural politics," no genuinely political struggle for cultural authority. The second is that the link between theory and practice is destroyed. The upshot, then, is that both culture and theory are "depoliticized." Meanwhile, Rorty's politics "assumes an overly communitarian and solidary character" (266).

It is indeed paradoxical, Fraser points out, that a thinker who appeals so often to the values of community and conversation should develop an increasingly monological position in relation to politics. But such is indeed the case with Richard Rorty. There is simply no place in his political scheme for those who speak something other than "the language of bourgeois liberalism." Rorty's "Partition" position thus "cuts out the ground for the possibility of democratic radical politics" (267).

In contrast to Rorty's liberal pragmatism, Fraser argues for "democratic-socialist-feminist-pragmatism" and formulates a "recipe" to further that political end. Her literary form is chosen, she remarks, with some deliberation. It "has a number of advantages, not least of which is a certain gender resonance" (Footnote 27, 271). Furthermore, the "recipe" form

> ... suggests a nontechnocratic and more genuinely pragmatic view of the relation between theory and practice since cooks are expected to vary recipes in accordance with trial and error, inspiration, and the conjunctural state of the larder. Finally, the recipe form has the advantage of positing the outcome as a concoction rather than a system. (271)

Importantly, Fraser begins her recipe with "a sort of zerodegree pragmatism" which she calls a "useful" but not sufficient ingredient for her "concoction." Like Cornel West and Richard Bernstein, then, Fraser draws on the pragmatic tradition but finds it necessary to modify and supplement it in the interest of creating a theoretically informed radical democratic politics.

Fraser's "democratic-socialist-feminist-pragmatism" entails a Gramscian critique of cultural hegemony and a radical challenge to Rorty's notion of solidarity as an intellectually and politically adequate alternative to objectivity. Contemporary society, Fraser observes, generates politically diverse communities, multiple solidarities, which compete within a "basic institutional framework." Within this framework, some communities and the vocabularies with which they describe the world are dominant, while others are subordinate. This relational quality of domination and subordination is not, even according to Rorty's own pragmatic logic, the consequence of "the nature of things." But neither is prevailing social reality the result of historical "accident," as Rorty sometimes implies. Rather, the competitive tension among politically diverse communities is played out within an institutional construct which works to "the systematic detriment of some social groups and to the systematic profit of others" (269).

As an illustration of Fraser's argument, consider the differences between her own description of social reality and that of Rorty or Bloom. Consider further that the roots of *prescription* in relation to social change are contained within *descriptions* of present social reality. In other words, genuine political contest begins once competing descriptions are developed or accepted. Fraser's description of contemporary society contains the following elements:

> an organization of social production for private profit rather than for human need; a gender-based division of social labor that separates privatized childrearing from recognized and remunerated work; gender and race-segmented paid labor markets that generate a marginalized underclass; a system of nation-states that engage in crisis-management in the form of segmented social-welfare concessions and subsidized war production. (269)

As Fraser indicates, her description of social reality characterizes the political understandings held in common by various "solidarities"—feminists, democratic-socialists, and some pragmatists. The vocabulary employed is fairly esoteric, suggesting that this is also the description of an academically trained intellectual. Assuming that Fraser is a professional philosopher and in a position to introduce her students to this vocabulary and to this description of social reality, she is an actor in what she understands as cultural politics. This does not mean, of course, that the college or university classroom is the only, or even primary, stage on which cultural politics is played out. But insofar as advanced industrial society offers few other outlets for professional philosophers except academia, Fraser fulfills her own concept of the intellectual as one who occupies a "specifiable location[s] in social space, rather than as [a] free-floating individual[s] who [is] beyond ideology" (270). She is the self-conscious embodiment of her own theory that intellectual life is inherently political, and her objective is democratic social transformation.

As I indicated at the outset of this discussion of Nancy Fraser's critique of Rorty, her views are consistent with those of others who have been historically voiceless, that is, traditionally marginalized by dominant philosophical and political theory and practice. This is an important theme, and one that I will pursue further in the final two chapters of this text. First, however, I want briefly to examine two other recent critiques of Rorty's work and to extend my comparison of Rorty and Camus.

Frank Lentricchia

Fraser's concept of the politically engaged intellectual is shared by literary critic Frank Lentricchia, who is also critical of Rorty, while agreeing with (as do many of Rorty's critics) his antifoundationalism. In his 1983 book, *Criticism and Social Change,* Lentricchia writes,

> With Richard Rorty, I am ready to set aside the classical claim of philosophy for representational adequacy. In its place, I am ready to urge (Rorty is not) a materialist view that theory does its representing with a purpose. This sort of theory seeks not to find the foundation and the conditions of truth, but to exercise power for the purpose of social change. It says that there is no such thing as eter-

nally 'true' theory. It says that theories are generated only
in history—no theory comes from outside—for the purpose
of generating more history in a certain way: generating the
history we want. (12)

Lentricchia's book, as well as his 1988 essay, "The 'Life' of a
Humanist Intellectual," centers on the sense of historical/po-
litical purpose, or more accurately, the *lack* thereof, experienced by today's academic humanists. In the book, Lentricchia applauds Rorty's rejection of "some natural
standpoint called 'reality'" that lends authority to the projects of humanist intellectuals. But he is critical of Rorty's
stark dualism: "either . . . a multi-voiced, uncoordinated cultural conversation or a representative 'reality' that demands
a single discourse and a single voice" (*Criticism* 16).

Missing from Rorty's analysis, writes Lentricchia, is "society." By injecting society into Rorty's scheme, one becomes
aware that the "conversation of culture" is not and has never
been as free as Rorty apparently believes or wishes. The
authority which both propels and constrains this conversation is social. Thus, "you cannot jump into this conversation
and do what you please" (16). Not only participation in the
conversation but also the character of participation after
admittance are subject to social authority.

Lentricchia argues that while Rorty celebrates the "liberal personal needs" honored in traditional literary culture,
he does not address the character of the society which represses those needs and their fulfillment. But on the other
hand, Lentricchia interprets Rorty's "critical aestheticism"
as a reaction to the repressive character "of a culture that
must toe the line of a natural standpoint" (17). "[O]nly if
[Rorty] first believe[d] that our old social being [was] at the
root unsatisfying," writes Lentricchia, would he propose the
flight of individuals from the "normalizing" culture which
helped to shape that old social being. In other words, it is for
the sake of the social that Rorty proposes "edifying" or
"therapeutic" philosophy over against "that old-time philosophy." But it is far from evident, Lentricchia maintains
(along with Fraser), that the pleasures of creativity and
imagination contribute to a new and better social being. In

fact, Lentricchia argues that Rorty's stress on the original and creative plays into the hands of late capitalism, an economic structure wherein "the Romantic yearning for the new is . . . transformed into an energetic consumerism" (18).

According to Lentricchia, then, Rorty perceives the "unsatisfying" character of our "old social being" and proposes, for the purpose of social change, a flight into a literary culture which once possessed a degree of critical power, as when individuals such as Wordsworth employed it against early industrial capitalism. But Rorty's desire for solidarity, however genuine, cannot be fulfilled by appealing to this form of literary culture *now* because late capitalism has appropriated Romantic literary values for its own perpetuation. The time is simply past, Lentricchia argues, for any "critical rhetoric which isolates the aesthetic from our political and social lives" (19).

Rorty's vision of culture, divorced as it is from political power, is "the leisured vision of liberalism: the free pursuit of personal growth anchored in material security" (18). This vision, Lentricchia declares, has run its course as a device of critical/utopian rhetoric. And such rhetoric is vital for those academic humanists who would "make a contribution to the formation of a community different from the one we live in" (19).

Lentricchia's purpose in *Criticism and Social Change* is to show that while "not all social power is literary power . . . all literary power is social power" (19). This marks his point of departure from Rorty, who, in the final analysis, does not alleviate and even contributes to the moral and political "paralysis" which grips humanist intellectuals and which Lentricchia has deplored throughout the past decade. I will return to his general critique in the final section of this chapter.

Henry Giroux

The themes articulated by Rorty's left-wing critics— West, Bernstein, Fraser, and Lentricchia—are similar, despite the diversity of their approaches. Henry Giroux, another critic of Rorty, summarizes these themes nicely.

> In Rorty's perspective, the intellectual is reduced to simply being a somewhat privileged member of the community in the service of conversation, a member without a politics, a sense of vision, or a conscience. What is most striking about Rorty's view of conversation and community is the idealized pluralism that it supports. Treated as simply conventions, rather than as social practices that take place within asymmetrical relations of power, the notion of conversation is imbued with a false equality that glides over the issue of how specific interests and power relations actually structure the material and ideological conditions in which conversations are actually structured. Who is in the conversation? Who controls the terms of the dialogue? Who is left out? What interests are sustained beyond the abstract virtue of Socratic dialogue? Whose stories are distorted or marginalized? Why are some parts of the conversation considered more important than others? How does one decide between competing visions of community life as they are embodied in different strands of the conversation? (*Schooling* 64)

Giroux maintains that in ignoring these questions, Rorty "provides a version of postmodern philosophy that is fundamentally anti-utopian."

> [I]t ultimately ends up offering no ethical or political grounds on which either to challenge the human suffering and contradictions inherent in modern society or to exhibit the moral and political courage necessary to struggle for a society without exploitation. (65)

Giroux's charge that Rorty offers neither a "language of hope" nor "a language of critique" echoes themes developed by West, Bernstein, Fraser, and Lentricchia, all of whom fault Rorty for offering—in Bernstein's phrase—"little more than an *apologia* for the status quo" (541). What Giroux identifies as Rorty's "anti-utopianism" is related, I believe, to the charge leveled by the other critics discussed here that

Rorty strips radical intellectuals of any social and political function.

Rorty and Camus on Human Nature and Utopia: A Contrast

In this context, it seems fair to assert the following: Rorty is much more concerned with what "we" who live in the First-World liberal democracies have to lose than he is with what "we" might hope to create in the future, and for that matter, the present. *"Nothing,"* he declares, "is more important than the preservation of these liberal institutions," referring to the free press, an independent judiciary, and the modern university ("Thugs" 567). By the same token, he is apparently motivated more by a fear of those who envision and attempt to enforce totalizing or absolute utopias (Platonist/Reactionaries, Marxists/Leninists, Christian "reconstructionists," etc.) than he is by moral outrage or despair over the way things are in the social/political present. Add to these two related factors Rorty's claims that liberal conscience and culture are the accidental products of various historical developments and that progress can be identified only in retrospect, and the judgments of his left-wing critics seem fair and reasonable.

Basic to this issue is Rorty's characteristically postmodern "decentering of the subject" and his insistence that democracy requires no particular view of the self. This orientation separates his philosophical project from those of both his conservative and radical critics. With no particular human image to nurture and defend, Rorty vexes both old-style humanists, who charge him with nihilism and relativism, and modern progressive radicals, who accuse him of conservative apologetics and "anti-utopianism."

Two key questions emerge here: (1) Is it possible to maintain a theory of human nature that does not marginalize the "other" (anyone who deviates theoretically)? And, (2) Do utopian visions inevitably result in authoritarian politics? In the remainder of this chapter I intend to support an affirmative answer to the first of these questions and a negative response to the second. In so doing, I will indicate my own misgivings about Rorty's postmodernist project.

While I deplore the tactics of Allan Bloom and others who employ a natural metaphysics to justify elitist social and political projects, and while I am sympathetic with Rorty's view that the practice of democracy is prior to philosophy, I am nonetheless more concerned than is Rorty with what I take as the universal human struggle against meaninglessness, which he appears to dismiss as simply the sediment of foundational philosophy. My argument is that while the demise of foundational philosophy certainly represents the passing of one particular cultural response to the existential need for what he calls "metaphysical comfort," the need itself is no less powerful. Furthermore, insofar as this need entails a natural demand for meaning and dignity, and insofar as this need is fulfilled by culture, the ethical character of cultural institutions takes on vital significance.

This is not to say, as Bloom does, that one must get outside of the cultural "cave" to judge the ethical validity of the cultural means of achieving dignity and meaning. Rather, I understand that the ethical critique emanates from embodied seekers of dignity and meaning, who also manifest particular and diverse experiences, histories, and political relationships.

Rorty, I believe, emphasizes the latter (the cultural dimensions of the self) at the expense of the former (the embodied natural demand for dignity and meaning). This imbalance contributes, in my reading, to what Giroux calls Rorty's "fundamentally anti-utopian" attitude. While I agree with Giroux, I see theoretically richer possibilities in Lentricchia's characterization of Rorty's "curiously truncated" utopianism.

In this context, I find helpful a distinction made by Paul Tillich between the "utopian spirit" and "absolutized utopia." For Tillich, the "utopian spirit" springs from a universal human desire for wholeness and community. In this sense, "utopia" is synonymous with absolute or perfect moral unity, but the content of the utopian symbol, the character of the moral community, varies according to particular ideologies and influences or even determines human attitudes and behaviors. However, regardless of particular and diverse utopian symbols, the universal need for wholeness and community points to a moral (social and political) standard. Despair over the way things are is an acknowledgement of moral failure, and any thinker who posits some sort of corrective, however minimal, to the way things are is manifesting what Tillich calls the "utopian spirit." In other words, to conceive of something better in relation to human wholeness and community is an inherently utopian project.

But Tillich argues further that there is an important difference between the "utopian spirit," which springs from a universal human need for wholeness and community, and absolutized utopia. The former, as Tillich points out, seeks *ever new* possibilities for unity, while the latter inevitably requires defense, usually to the point of force. In this context, Tillich writes, "It is the spirit of utopia that conquers utopia" ("Critique" 309).

The utopian projects of Plato and the Hebrew prophets help to illustrate Tillich's distinction. While both exhibit the "utopian spirit," the content of their respective visions differs radically. Plato, troubled by diversity or the problem of "the one and the many," conceives of a utopian society which requires indoctrination, deception, even force for its perpetuation and protection. The prophets, on the other hand, subsume diversity under a prior commitment to equality. Therefore, their social ideal is intrinsically anti-absolutistic in that they envision an end which is morally inseparable from, and is in fact justified only by, the means of achieving it. (This is a vital difference, and I will consider its implications more thoroughly in the following chapter.)

My understanding is that Rorty does not make the distinction elucidated by Tillich, and that this constitutes an important shortcoming in his work. For example, it is one thing to reject philosophies which provide ideological justifications for absolutized utopias, but quite another to deny the implications of a universally human utopian spirit.

The former points to an admirable commitment to democracy. The latter, however, entails a rejection of the necessity
to critique the specific moral content of competing utopian
visions, and to analyze the reasons why some visions are
historically realized while others are not.

In connection with Tillich's distinction and with Lentricchia's argument that Rorty's "edifying philosophy" has a
"curiously truncated" utopian character, my reading is that
Rorty's project is utopian in spirit insofar as he recognizes
the "unsatisfying" character of contemporary social arrangements, and hopes that changing the way people think will
make us, as individuals, more tolerant, less cruel. This
squares with Tillich's claim that the utopian spirit springs
from the natural human desire for wholeness and community and is thus necessarily social. Rorty's commitment to an
open-ended democracy and his corresponding fear of absolutized utopia prevent him from going further, from endorsing
specific institutional transformation. In fact, he sees existing liberal institutions as vital safeguards against absolutized utopia.

The key social and political issue here is whether or not
kinder and more tolerant individuals, confined within the
structures of existing liberal institutions, could create a
"kinder and gentler" society. Rorty believes that they could.
Those to the left of him, including Lentricchia, think otherwise.

In the opening chapter of *Criticism and Social Change,*
Lentricchia points to the "polemical core" of his book by
referring to a distinction made by John Dewey and picked up
by Kenneth Burke. (The latter is a central figure in Lentricchia's study.) "The distinction," Lentricchia writes, "is
between 'education as a function of society' and 'society as a
function of education'" (1).

> In the end, that is a way of dividing the world between
> those who like it and those who do not. If you are at home
> in society, you will accept it, and you will want education
> to perform the function of preparing the minds of the
> young and the not-so-young to maintain society's prin-

ciples and directives. . . . If you hold such a theory of education, you are a conservative. Insofar as you think the order
should be reversed, that society should be a function of
education, you are a radical, or that strange, impossible
utopian, the radical in reverse gear we call a reactionary.
(To complete the picture: liberals, in this scheme, are nervous conservatives governed by an irresistible impulse to
tinker, though when the chips are down, they usually find
a way to resist their need to mess with the machine.) The
radical of either the progressive or the nostalgic type is not
at home in society; the radical feels alienated and dis-
possessed. As Burke puts it: "To say that 'society' should be
a function of 'education' is to say, in effect, that the principles and directives of the prevailing society are radically
askew . . . and that education must serve to remake it ac-
cordingly." (1–2)

It is, I believe, quite clear where Allan Bloom fits into
the Dewey-Burke-Lentricchia distinction. Bloom, the "nostalgic radical," is far from "at home" in society and believes
so fully in "society as a function of education" that he fore-
sees the end of Western civilization itself unless higher
education is radically changed.

It is also clear where Rorty's left-wing critics (including
Lentricchia himself) fit. Their shared insistence that academic humanists perform a particular social and political
function, that such individuals need to break out of their
"moral paralysis" and take sides in a society now characterized, as West maintains, by "racism . . . , patriarchy . . . ,
class inequality . . . , state repression . . . , and technological
abuse of nature"—these are all indicative of their progressive radical persuasion.

And where does Richard Rorty fit? Insofar as his cru-
sade against foundational philosophy is an example of "tin-
kering" while the social machine remains intact, Rorty is a
"nervous conservative," a liberal. Moreover, this description
characterizes many, perhaps even most, contemporary
North American academics—decent and well-meaning men
and women whose intellectual energies are confined to the
problems which exist on the "cutting edge" of their individ-

ual disciplines, and whose relationships with society beyond the walls of the university are either fairly comfortable, or so distant as to preclude meaningful engagement, or both. If my reading is correct, then the reasons for Rorty's "curiously truncated" utopian spirit (and that of many other contemporary intellectuals) need to be traced beyond antifoundational philosophical views and into the very structure of institutional life in the United States.

While Rorty's philosophical project is at its best a thorough rejection of any ideological justification for absolutized utopia, he is not willing to deal with the full implications of a universally human utopian spirit and its curious truncation in contemporary U.S. society. In fact, I think that he would argue that this spirit is not natural, but cultural—related to specific historical and linguistic forms—and in need of moderation for the purpose of averting "cultural disaster." Implied by this reading is a fear that the utopian spirit, thoroughly unleashed, would lead first to anarchy and then, inevitably, to repressive, totalizing utopia (which, strangely enough, smacks of Plato's distrust of democracy). But among Rorty's critics are those who claim that this need not be the case. These persons envision new possibilities for wholeness and community, new social arrangements that are more responsive to the universal need for dignity and meaning. In many instances, these thinkers see the liberal institutions which Rorty so deeply reveres as, in Noam Chomsky's words, "ideological [agents] that channel thought and attitudes within acceptable bounds, deflecting any potential challenge to established privilege and authority before it can take form and gather strength" (Preface).

Among the issues left unresolved in this critique of Rorty is the moral basis on which particular historical and social manifestations of the universally human utopian spirit might be judged. In other words, assuming that various elements of competing utopian visions are realized within social structures, that most history is not "accidental," but in fact proceeds out of the utopian spirit of embodied actors with diverse and particular political identities, is there any basis for moral judgment, including judgment that cuts across the bounds of competing political communities and institutions? This is, of course, the issue which plagues all of the thinkers reviewed in this book. My own sense is that a further comparison between Rorty and Camus is a helpful way to begin addressing this vital question, beyond the Platonic realism of Bloom (which provides justification for absolutized utopia) and the apolitical pragmatic liberalism of Rorty (which evades the implications of the utopian spirit).

In chapter 3 I compared Richard Rorty with Albert Camus and indicated that one of their several similarities is the harsh criticism directed at both from the political left. In an earlier study, I argued that this criticism was not altogether justified in the case of Camus (Warehime 72). It is more difficult, if not impossible, for me to defend Rorty in the same way. The reason for this difficulty is twofold: (1) Camus, unlike Rorty, consistently maintained his belief in "something" within human nature which "rejects the order of things" (*L'Homme Révolté* 641), and (2) again unlike Rorty, Camus continually affirmed, "against the abstractions of history, that which transcends all history, and *which is flesh . . . " (Essais* 406) (emphasis added). In other words, Camus presents a view of human nature which integrates the "utopian spirit" with the givenness of corporeality.

Out of this understanding, Camus develops an ethical sensibility which I believe is prophetic in character. By this I mean that, like the Hebrew prophets, Camus presents an intrinsically anti-absolutistic utopian vision which judges history and human action within it in the name of the "something" which transcends history. In the precritical culture of ancient Israel, this "something" was Yahweh, who symbolized that which is immortal and commands human loyalty. In Camusian terms, this "something" is the natural human refusal to be reduced to an object, the corresponding rejection of "the order of things," and the bodily reality which remains an eternal given. For Camus, as for the prophets, these aspects of human life are inseparable, so that—as one

Camus scholar puts it—"what counts as a criterion of action and judgment is what happens to the lives of men and women regarded as the flesh and blood beings which they are" (Pierce 127). From this it follows that "justice has to do with what happens to people's bodies" (127).

I maintain that Camus points to a theory of human nature which does not marginalize "the other" and which manifests the "utopian spirit" while simultaneously guarding against absolutized utopias. This not only represents an important departure from Rorty (and from Bloom, too, of course) but also provides a basis on which competing utopian visions may be analyzed and judged. This basis is directly related to a keen awareness of dehumanization, defined as the imposition of bodily and existential suffering, even to the point of destruction. Simply stated, any utopian ideal which suppresses the natural human desire for ever new possibilities for wholeness and unity and smothers the natural human tendency to "reject the order of things" in the interest of human dignity and meaning is inevitably a totalizing utopia which entails selective dehumanization, selective suffering, selective destruction.

Significantly, neither Bloom (who insists on the reality of universal human nature) nor Rorty (who, with equal determination, rejects such reality) demonstrates moral outrage with institutionalized dehumanization. Those who have encountered this dehumanization are rightfully suspicious of both Bloom's and Rorty's concepts of democracy and of their philosophies of self.

I believe that Camus, who explicitly rejects the role of philosopher, nonetheless presents the starting point for a critical analysis of institutionalized dehumanization. By locating human value in an essentially bodily reality, Camus retains—if somewhat paradoxically—what is best in postmodern philosophy's historicism, while also providing a quasi-metaphysical grounds for social and political critique. The utopian spirit, which is born anew in each finite human being, points to the equation (drawn by Robert McAfee Brown) of a "moral society" with a "perpetually unfinished" society.

In the following chapter, I will develop this theme more fully, drawing primarily on the work of Cornel West and considering the understanding of moral authority contained within his "prophetic pragmatism," as well as its implications for democracy and education.

CHAPTER FIVE

Prophetic Pragmatism
and Education for
Creative Democracy

But the fact is not that the Negro has no tradition but that there has as yet arrived no sensibility sufficiently profound and tough to make this tradition articulate. For a tradition expresses, after all, nothing more than the long and painful experience of a people; it comes out of the battle waged to maintain their integrity or, to put it more simply, out of their struggle to survive.

—James Baldwin

Ideas—religious, moral, practical, aesthetic—must, as Max Weber, among others, never tired of insisting, be carried by powerful social groups to have powerful social effects; someone must revere them, celebrate them, defend them, impose them. They have to be institutionalized in order to find not just an intellectual existence in society, but, so to speak, a material one as well.

—Clifford Geertz

Call it upward mobility
But you've been sold down the river
Just another form of slavery

And the whole man-made white world
Is your master

—Tracy Chapman*

Introduction

In this chapter, I will explore various works by Cornel West, who shares Camus's prophetic spirit, but attempts to support its ethical demands much more theoretically than Camus thought possible. West's critique of Rorty was treated in the preceding chapter. Here, I intend to consider his writing in broader context and to present his "prophetic pragmatism" as a challenging and hopeful alternative to the philosophical and political views analyzed thus far in my study. Once again, the notion of moral authority will be a central theme.

Like Camus, West draws explicitly on his own experience and acknowledges its shaping influence on his philosophical and political orientation. Unlike Camus, West self-consciously draws upon the prophetic tradition for moral sustenance, develops Marxist-informed theories with which to critique Western culture, and advocates specific political practices aimed at particular social consequences.

Cornel West: The Prophetic Tradition

Central to West's perspective is his role as an Afro-American intellectual with radical political affinities. These affinities, he argues, are of a piece with "prophetic Christian thought," which is

---

... guided by a profound conception of human nature and human history, a persuasive picture of what one is as a person, what one should hope for, and how one ought to act. (*Prophesy* 16)

Thus, West explains, his experience in the black prophetic church is a major source of his philosophical and political outlook. Importantly, the prophetic tradition keeps faith with "the capacity of human beings to transform their circumstances," engages in relentless social and self criticism, and projects "visions, analyses, and practices of social freedom" ("Prophetic Tradition" 38).

Consistent with this understanding is West's perception of his philosophical project as "an exercise in critical self-inventory, as a historical, social, and existential situating of [his] work as an intellectual activist, and human being" (*Evasion* 7). Motivated, he confesses, by disenchantment with intellectual life in America" and by "demoralization regarding the political and cultural state of the country," West understands his role of humanist intellectual as inherently ethical and political and his objective as one of social transformation (7–8).

In addition to prophetic Christianity, West draws upon both progressive Marxism and pragmatism to delineate the character and responsibilities of "Afro-American critical thought," a delineation which he sees as especially important in that "American philosophy has never taken the Afro-American experience seriously" (*Prophesy Deliverance* 11). All of these traditions, he is quick to point out, are vulnerable to vulgarization and distortion and, in fact, have been historically subjected to such on a grand scale. Nevertheless, he perceives each of the three as a vital contribution to "the last humane hope for humankind" in view of the profound "international and domestic crises we now face" (*Prophesy Deliverance* 96; *Evasion* 8). In the following section of this chapter, I will discuss West's analysis of these three philosophical traditions, their common ethical, cultural, and political concerns, and their implications for intellectual life in the interest of creative democracy.

Analysis: *Prophesy Deliverance!:* "Sources and Tasks of Afro-American Critical Thought"

West's most thorough discussions of prophetic Christianity, progressive Marxism, and American pragmatism are contained in two books: *Prophesy Deliverance!* (1982) and *The American Evasion of Philosophy* (1989). In the former, he spells out the "sources and tasks of Afro-American critical thought" (15–24). Importantly, West identifies prophetic Christianity and pragmatism as the two dominant *sources* of such thought, while a "dialogical encounter" with progressive Marxist social analysis is named as a vital *task*. In the 1989 book, West weaves the three traditions into a form of cultural critique which he calls "prophetic pragmatism." My discussion will draw from both of these publications, as well as from a few shorter pieces.

As indicated above, the first dominant source of Afro-American critical thought identified by West is prophetic Christianity, at the core of which is the conviction that "every individual . . . should have the opportunity to fulfill his or her potentialities" (*Prophesy Deliverance* 16). The prophetic tradition stresses the equal worth of all persons before a transcendent God and thus contributes to both a radical egalitarianism and a staunch commitment to the dignity of all persons. The prophetic concept of dignity, furthermore, is inseparable from a belief in the common human "ability to contradict what is, to change . . . and to act in the light of that which is not-yet" (17). Decision, commitment, engagement, and action are thus central values. However, this concept of human dignity is held in dialectical tension with a notion of human depravity, defined by West as the "proclivity to cling to the moment, to refuse to transform and be transformed" (17). Thus, while "the furtherance of the uncertain quest for human freedom" is a historical good, absolute perfection is an impossibility.

According to West, the prophetic ideal of freedom is twofold: existential and social. The former is that which sustains individuals through personal crises (death, despair) and empowers them for social freedom, the aim of prophetic collective practice. Related to both kinds of freedom is the concept of democracy, which is of a piece with the prophetic commitment to "the self-realization of human individuality within community" (18–19). Moreover, the meaning of democracy is linked with the notion of dignity, the potential for "human betterment." Thus, West explains, the prophetic dialectic of human nature and history makes democracy "necessary and possible," while the praxis of imperfect human beings makes it "desirable and realizable" (19).

West maintains, then, that prophetic Afro-American Christian thought concentrates not only on "the existential anxiety, political oppression, economic exploitation, and social degradation of human beings," but simultaneously on human possibility, the potential to transform "prevailing realities" and to create "that which is not-yet." In this way, such thought is characterized by an awareness of the tragedy of human history but also by a dedication to "the struggle for freedom and the spirit of hope" (19–20).

The second source of Afro-American critical thought named by West is American pragmatism, especially the work of John Dewey, who "recognized that philosophy is inextricably bound to culture, society, and history" (20). Critical interpretation of the past and critical scrutiny of earlier interpretations in the light of present experience are thus the central activities of pragmatism, while its objective is to solve "specific problems presently confronting the cultural way of life from which people come" (20). For pragmatists, the pursuit of knowledge is transformed from "a private affair" into a communal inquiry, and knowledge claims are secured by social practice rather than "the purely mental activity of an individual subject" (20–21). Furthermore, dialogical interpretation of "prevailing communal practices" is directed toward transformation of "existing realities." Importantly, because no social norm, premise, or procedure is understood as the consequence of some objective order of things, pragmatism demythologizes "the myth of the given" (20–21). The process of communal dialogue is perennial, self-correcting, and guided not by "the quest for certainty" but rather by "moral convictions" and the "search for desirable and realizable historical possibilities" (21).

While West is generally admiring of pragmatism, he also points to its major shortcomings:

> . . . its relative neglect of the self, its refusal to take class struggle seriously, and its veneration of scientific method and the practices of the scientific community. (21)

In view of these shortcomings, pragmatism needs prophetic Christianity's emphasis on "the uniqueness of human personality." Furthermore, both pragmatism and prophetic Christianity require the additional awareness that is made possible by progressive (not orthodox or scientific) Marxist social analysis. This additional awareness is twofold: "the centrality of the class struggle, and the political dimensions of knowledge" (21).

Thus, a major task for Afro-American critical thought is to enter into dialogue with progressive Marxism. This dialogue begins with the recognition of a "fundamental similarity" shared by progressive Marxism, prophetic Christianity, and critically modified pragmatism:

> . . . commitment to the negation of what is, and the transformation of prevailing realities in the light of the norms of individuality and democracy. (101)

The major contribution of progressive Marxism to Afro-American critical thought is a theoretical means to critique late capitalist society, "the way in which the existing system of production and the social structure relate to black oppression and exploitation" (111). Such a theoretical framework is necessary, writes West, for "the emergence of any substantive political program or social vision" (111).

Without a Marxist-informed theoretical approach, notions of racial liberation consist simply "of including black people within the mainstream of liberal capitalist America." Such notions thus equate "liberation" with "middle-class status" rather than with tangible participation "in the decision-making processes that regulate [people's] lives" (112). These notions, then, are grossly inadequate. For West:

> [d]emocratic control over the institutions in the productive and political processes in order for them to satisfy human needs and protect personal liberties of the populace constitutes human liberation. (112)

In other words, without a social theory which clarifies "what people must be liberated from," Afro-American critical thought cannot "present an idea of liberation with socioeconomic content" (111–12). And liberation without such content is not genuine liberation at all because it lacks any meaningful understanding of what constitutes power and powerlessness in American society.

A middle-class salary, West contends, is not synonymous with social power. Rather, as Marxist social theory shows:

> [P]ower in modern industrial society consists of a group's participation in the decision-making processes of the major institutions that affect their destinies. . . . Only collective power over the major institutions of society [institutions of production and production flow] constitutes genuine power on behalf of the people. (114)

In liberal capitalist America, however, such institutions are largely controlled by

> . . . multinational corporations that monopolize production in the marketplace and prosper partially because of . . . public support in the form of government subsidies, free technological equipment, lucrative contracts, and sometimes even direct transfer payments. (113)

While racism *intensifies* the powerlessness of Afro-Americans, it does not, in and of itself, *create* such powerlessness. Indeed, the vast majority of American citizens share the same impotence in that

[t]hey have no substantive control over their lives, little
participation in the decision-making process of the major
institutions that regulate their lives. (114–15)

Despite his contention that Afro-American critical
thought devoid of Marxist social theory is inadequate, West
does not believe that social oppression can be fully accounted
for in the traditional terms of class analysis. Rather, he
maintains that "cultural and religious attitudes, values, and
sensibilities have a life and logic of their own" (116). Here,
then, he appeals to the cultural analysis of Antonio Gramsci
(whose intellectual influence is apparent in Stanley Aronowitz's critique of Bloom and in Nancy Fraser's "recipe" for
"democratic-socialist-feminist-pragmatism.")

West calls Gramsci "the most penetrating Marxist theorist of culture in this century" (118). For Gramsci, West
explains, "class struggle is not simply the battle between . . . owners and producers in the work situation."
Rather,

[i]t also takes the form of cultural and religious conflicts
over which attitudes, values, and beliefs will dominate the
thought and behavior of people. (119)

The subtlety of this conflict becomes apparent when one
realizes that no society or state is sustained exclusively by
force; rather, every society requires the legitimation that is
formed in the cultural arena where "everyday life is felt,
outlooks formed, and self-images adopted" (119). The dominant cluster of these images, sensibilities, and ideas "supports and sanctions the existing order," thus exercising what
Gramsci calls "hegemony" over other oppositional cultural
attitudes, which exist subterraneously or marginally. A
"hegemonic culture" thrives as long as it can perpetuate its
own self-legitimation. But its authority crumbles when previously buried or peripheral attitudes and sensibilities cap-
ture the hearts and minds of greater numbers of people, who
then present a "counter-hegemonic" threat to the dominant
culture.

Gramsci's Theory of Hegemony:
Platonic and Prophetic Roots

To draw out some of the implications of Gramsci's theory, it may be helpful to recall the moral challenge presented in the 1960s to the institutions which claimed to embody and defend the values of democracy and the distinctions drawn in the Preface to this study between Platonic and prophetic notions of moral authority. For example, both the Platonic roots and the pragmatic dimensions of Gramsci's cultural analysis are apparent in book 2 of *The Republic,* wherein Socrates and Adeimantus discuss the divine image which will be permitted in the education of the guardians. In this section, Socrates' concern is not theological, but social and political. His aim is to create a harmonious social order. Toward that same end, he proposes in book 3 the "noble lie" (or the "myth of the metals") which will preclude any challenges to the caste system because it will be perceived as a creation of the god, a given.

While Plato, of course, was no democrat, he unveils the noble lie as just that—a lie. Readers of *The Republic* know that the utopia it describes is a thoroughly human creation. Thus, *The Republic* shows how hegemony works. It illustrates Gramsci's claim that "[e]very relationship of hegemony is necessarily an educational relationship" (*Notebooks* 350). Plato's Socrates knows that once the status quo is established, it must be protected, and Plato is quite willing to reveal the necessary cultural means. If a just society is synonymous with an orderly, stable, and rigidly hierarchical society, such means are acceptable.

But Plato, to repeat the well-known point, was no democrat, even by ancient standards. His utopian model in *The Republic* allows for a limited and well-managed diversity, but not for social and political equality, regardless of whether that concept is understood as a natural law or as a humanly created ideal.

The roots of democratic equality, as Cornel West indicates, are far more apparent in the prophetic tradition. For the prophets, equality is a moral imperative which requires human activity for realization, but it is neither a humanly created ideal nor a natural law. Whereas Greek philosophers tended to look to nature to systematize social and cultural diversity and to define justice, the Hebrews looked beyond both nature and culture to Yahweh, a "mysterious power who entered the world at will but was never bound to any of its forms" as the source of morality itself (Schneidau 64). For the prophets, social and cultural diversity was subsumed under the imperative of equality. To paraphrase Jeremiah, to know Yahweh is to do justice. In other words, anyone who lives in a manner which affirms equality, justice, and compassion "knows" Yahweh. Such knowing is not restricted to the Hebrews; even and sometimes *especially* the "stranger" lives a knowing life. Thus, the central moral imperative of living justly, mercifully, and humbly supersedes any problem of diversity.

The real issue for the prophets is that of power. Those who enjoy the benefits of social inequality are not likely to participate in the dismantling of the structures which ensure their own comfort and prestige. They are far more likely to rationalize their superiority and authority, and if the less powerful can be convinced of the validity of this rationalization, then hegemony is established. The prophets, however, are never convinced. Instead, they continually insist that any social arrangement in which equality, justice, and compassion are not central is not "of Yahweh," but is idolatrous and in desperate need of change. Furthermore, such change requires human participation in history with Yahweh.

The prophets, it should be pointed out, *want* hegemonic status. They want to educate their society, to mold it in a certain way, by instilling particular attitudes and behaviors. But while there always exists a potential for prophetic justice, there is also something which always works against it (as Cornel West indicates). Thus the prophetic model itself reveals the impossibility of prophetic hegemony. Prophetic discourse remains perpetually counter-hegemonic, a language of critique and a language of hope.

As indicated earlier, the character of and struggle for cultural hegemony (or authority) is apparent in the civil rights movement of the 1960s. A poignant example is Martin Luther King's "Letters from Birmingham Jail."

> I have traveled the length and breadth of Alabama, Mississippi and all the other southern states. On sweltering summer days and crisp autumn mornings I have looked at the South's beautiful churches with their lofty spires pointing heavenward. I have beheld the impressive religious-education buildings. Over and over I have found myself asking: "What kind of people worship here? Who is their God? Where were their voices when the lips of Governor Barnett dripped with words of interposition and nullification? Where were they when Governor Wallace gave a clarion call for defiance and hatred? Where were their voices of support when bruised and weary Negro men and women decided to rise from the dark dungeons of complacency to the bright hills of creative protest? (90–91)

King ponders the attitudes and behaviors of persons who would have barred him or any other African-American from entering the doors of their churches, inside of which they worshiped a god that he did not know; the attitudes and behaviors of persons who donned hooded robes on Saturday night and choir robes on Sunday morning; the attitudes and behaviors of persons who claimed loyalty to the same gospel as he and yet refused "to set at liberty those who are oppressed" (Luke 4:18).

A prophetic thinker, King recognizes the power of Platonist hegemony to rationalize inequality and to mask social/ethical contradictions. A powerful illustration of this same point is West's "genealogy of racism" (*Prophesy Deliverance*) which shows how the classical concepts of beauty and Enlightenment science together have exercised hegemony in the modern West, have merged to legitimate racial inequality in an "enlightened" culture.

West's Genealogy of Racism: A Confirmation of Gramsci's Theory

"The notion that black people are human beings is a relatively new discovery in the modern West," West declares.

> The idea of black equality in beauty, culture, and intellec-
> tual capacity remains problematic and controversial with-
> in prestigious halls of learning and sophisticated intellec-
> tual circles. The Afro-American encounter with the modern
> world has been shaped first and foremost by the doctrine of
> white supremacy, which is embodied in institutional prac-
> tices and enacted in everyday folkways under varying cir-
> cumstances and evolving conditions. (*Prophesy* 47)

For West, the legitimation of racism in modern history proceeded out of the uniquely Western "quest for truth and
knowledge" and the particular logic which characterized and
guided this quest. Scientific research principles, Cartesian
epistemology, and classical aesthetic ideals were fused in the
quest, which produced distinctive forms of "rationality,
scientificity, and objectivity" (47). These forms were highly
successful in perpetuating their own legitimacy, and in simultaneously prohibiting "the . . . legitimacy of the idea of
black equality in beauty, culture, and intellectual capacity"
(48). In other words, West maintains that "the structure of
modern discourse," that is, the "controlling metaphors, notions, categories, and norms" that have shaped (and continue
to shape) Western conceptions of truth and knowledge, was
determined by the self-legitimating claims of Enlightenment
science and philosophy, together with the modern revival of
the classical ideals of beauty, proportion, and moderation.

The scientific revolution, West explains, "set the framework for the advent of modernity" by bringing together two
ideas associated with research, namely, observation and evidence, and establishing them as the dominant paradigm of
knowledge (50). These research principles and their related
concepts such as hypothesis, inference, verification, and so
on, still undergird the authority of science. Francis Bacon
and Rene Descartes, particularly the latter, contributed to
this authority by providing a theoretical basis for its legitimacy. Descartes's project was to prove

> . . . that the fruits of scientific research do not merely prov-
> ide more useful ways for humans to *cope* with reality; such
> research also yields a true *copy* of reality. (51)

Hence the link between modern science and Cartesian epistemology, a link which depended largely on and renewed the legitimacy of "Greek ocular metaphors" (such as "Mind as Mirror of Nature" and "Eye of the Mind").

To this fusion of science and philosophy, West adds the modern recovery of classical antiquity, with what he calls its "normative gaze." By this he means "an ideal from which to order and compare observations" (53–54). Classical aesthetic norms and the scientific aims of observation, comparison, and measurement thus provided the synthesis upon which modern discourse developed. One of the first developments was a new authoritative discipline, natural history, which classified animal and human bodies according to visible characteristics. "These characteristics permit one to discern identity and difference, equality and inequality, beauty and ugliness . . . " (55).

Borrowing from both Michel Foucault and Ashley Montagu, West argues that the "descriptive, representational, order-imposing aims of natural history" led to the very concept of race (55). Moreover, the "normative gaze" of the classical revival led to evaluation and, thus, to an "implicit hierarchy" which ranked—on a scale presumed to be objective—the superior visage and character of white Europeans.

Quoting from and summarizing the records of early naturalists Francois Bernier, Carolus Linnaeus, and Georges Louis Leclerc de Buffon, West reveals their common tendency to view "Homo Europaeus" as the human norm. Buffon, for example, held that white was "the real and natural color of man" and that persons of other colors were "variations." He did allow, however, that "he unfortunate negroes . . . possess the seeds of every human virtue" and thus classified them within the human species (in West, 57). The descriptions of Linnaeus are also telling. Europeans, for example, are "gentle, acute, and inventive"; Africans are "crafty, indolent, negligent" (in West, 56). Moreover, Linnaeus apparently thought it appropriate to include remarks concerning the physique of African women, but not of Europeans, Americans, or Asians. And in the 1750s, when he theorized about the "hybridization of species," he restricted such unions to black women and male apes (56).

With the emergence of new disciplines connected with anthropology (phrenology and physiognomy), the European value-laden character of "scientific" observations became even more apparent. The Dutch anatomist, Pieter Camper, argued that "a beautiful face, beautiful body, beautiful nature, beautiful character, and beautiful soul were inseparable" (58). Associated with this claim was his chief "discovery," the "facial angle," which among Europeans averaged 97 degrees (relative to the ideal 100 degrees of ancient Greek sculpture), and which measured between 60 and 70 degrees for blacks, closer to the angle of apes and dogs (58). Even Johann Friedrich Blumenbach, who explicitly opposed hierarchical racial ranking, praised the "symmetrical face" as the most beautiful "because it approximated the 'divine' works of Greek art . . . specifically the proper anatomical proportions found in Greek sculpture" (57).

West indicates that many major thinkers of the Enlightenment (including Montesquieu, Voltaire, Hume, Kant, and Jefferson)

> . . . not merely held racist views, [but] also uncritically—during this age of criticism—believed that the *authority* for these views rested in the domain of naturalists, anthropologists, physiognomists, and phrenologists. (61)

Voltaire, for example, announced that

> . . . the Negro race is a species of men as different from ours as the breed of spaniels is from that of greyhounds. . . . [T]heir understanding . . . is greatly inferior. They are not capable of any great application or association of ideas . . . (in West, 61–62)

Meanwhile, Hume judged "the negroes, and in general all the other species of men" to be "naturally inferior to the whites," a claim he supported by pointing out that all civilization is the achievement of those with white complexion (62).

Kant, following Hume, maintained that the difference between blacks and whites "appears to be as great in regard to mental capacities as in color," and he wrote in a letter to an acquaintance who had reported to him the advice of a black person:

> It may be that there was something in this which perhaps deserved to be considered; but in short, this fellow was quite black from head to foot, a clear proof that what he said was stupid. (in West 63)

Finally, Jefferson determined that he could

> [n]ever . . . find that a black had uttered a thought above the level of plain narration; never see even an elementary trait of painting or sculpture. (in West 62)

From his "genealogy of modern racism," West concludes that

> . . . the everyday life of black people is shaped not simply by the exploitative (oligopolistic) capitalist system of production, but also by cultural attitudes and sensibilities . . . (65)

Although West does not specify a connection between his "genealogy" and Gramsci's notion of cultural hegemony, the former's inquiry is a poignant confirmation of the latter's theory. The cultural authority of science, Cartesian epistemology, and neoclassical aesthetic norms determined the character of the ideas and values of Enlightenment intellectuals and masked social/ethical contradictions which seem blatantly obvious in retrospect. Furthermore, as West points out, the "concrete effects" of the "structure of modern discourse"

> . . . continue to haunt the modern West: on the nondiscursive level, in ghetto streets, and on the discursive level, in methodological assumptions in the disciplines of the humanities. (48)

Cultural Hegemony and Humanities Education

If I understand him correctly, West alludes here to the professionalization and specialization of the modern humanities, a reflection of the hegemony of scientific research principles, and to the ethnocentrism of the canon, a reflection of the hegemony of white male European values and interests. This in turn points to the special problems encountered by Afro-American (and by inference, by anyone other than white male) humanist intellectuals who might challenge institutional norms. Furthermore, his argument points to the seemingly insurmountable hurdles faced by *any* oppositional or "counter-hegemonic" intellectual (white males included) whose objective is social criticism and transformation. On one hand, the postmodern emphasis on the contingency of language, which forms the basis of West's genealogy of racism, is itself a double-edged sword, in that it renders suspect the possibility of meaningful cultural critique. On the other hand, an entrenched structure of discrete academic disciplines precludes the necessary cooperative engagement of those who might challenge the cultural authority which supports various social practices, traditions, and structures.

This apparent deadlock, this crisis which affects not only the academy but, in West's estimation, the quality of human life throughout Western society, is related at its core to the possibility—or lack thereof—of human agency, both individual and collective, that is, the human capacity to envision new forms of democratic solidarity, to critique forces which obstruct that end, and to work with both determination and humility for social transformation. The crucial and unavoidable question for many humanist intellectuals is whether or not the academy provides a setting which fosters (or even permits) the search for new possibilities and the effectual criticism of forces which thwart those possibilities.

West himself has addressed this issue throughout the past decade, not only in his books, but also in such radical nonacademic journals as *Christianity and Crisis* and *Zeta*

Magazine. While his inquiry is most often directed specifically toward the intellectual and political crisis of Black America, he consistently argues that this crisis differs in intensity, but not in kind, from that facing the country as a whole. The need for genuine prophetic consciousness thus transcends race. For whites, blacks, and other nonwhites alike:

> [w]ithout a vibrant tradition of resistance for new generations, there can be no collective and critical consciousness—only professional conscientiousness. Without a vital community with precious ethical and religious ideals, there can be no moral commitment—only personal accomplishment. Without a credible sense of political struggle, there can be no courageous engagement—only cautious adjustment. ("The Crisis," *Zeta* 23)

The current decay in intellectual and political life, West believes, is more marked in the case of black humanist intellectuals than in that of whites, but the processes which characterize this decay are the same:

> ... the professionalization and specialization of knowledge, the bureaucratization of the academy, the proliferation of arcane jargon in the various disciplines, and the marginalization of humanistic studies. (24)

Applying to Black America an argument similar to Russell Jacoby's in *The Last Intellectuals,* West laments:

> For DuBois, the glorious life of the mind was a highly disciplined way of life and an intensely demanding way of struggle that facilitated transit between his study and the streets; whereas present-day Black scholars tend to be mere academicians, narrowly confined to specialized disciplines with little sense of the broader life of the mind and hardly any engagement with battles in the streets. (24)

Meanwhile, "the plight of the wretched of the earth deteriorates" (25).

What, Then, Is To Be Done? Prophetic Pragmatism, Traditions of Resistance, and Democracy

Most recently, West has advocated a form of cultural criticism which he calls "prophetic pragmatism" (*Evasion* 211ff.). Like Rorty, West returns to the pragmatic tradition, which is still, he argues, "the most influential stream in American thought" (212). But unlike Rorty, West envisions an explicitly political mode of criticism aimed at "promoting . . . creative democracy by means of critical intelligence and social action" (212).

For West, the "American evasion of philosophy" is a healthy rejection of Cartesian and Kantian epistemology, a rejection which began with Emerson and is apparent in the works of such diverse thinkers as C. Wright Mills, Reinhold Niebuhr, and W. E. B. DuBois, as well as Dewey, Peirce, and James. This rejection, West maintains, constituted "an assertion of the primacy of power-laden people's opinion (*doxa*) over value-free philosopher's knowledge (*episteme*)" (212).

Thus, North American intellectuals have at their disposal a philosophical tradition with rich political substance. This tradition does not require the elimination of professional elites, but it holds them accountable in a way in which they are not when "human potential and participation are suppressed in the name of . . . truth and knowledge" (212–13). This accountability points to the concept of democracy advocated by Benjamin Barber (and John Dewey before him), a form of "human relations." (Note the striking similarity between this concept of democracy and Weisel's declaration that "Jewish theology is human relations.") Moreover, it points to the need for "oppositional consciousness," which in turn requires the sustenance of traditions of resistance and struggle. Without such oppositional consciousness, the notion of accountability is empty.

Here it is appropriate to contrast West with such thinkers as Bennett and Bloom, who would also like to hold academic humanists accountable in the interest of democracy. West shows that holding academic humanists accountable to reproduce Platonist hegemonic culture lends itself not to democracy, but to a mind-controlling blindness to the social/ethical contradictions within that culture. Genuine democracy depends on dissent, which depends on oppositional consciousness, which depends on a sustained tradition of resistance, which depends on live "counter-hegemonic" communities. If the academic humanities are not—even cannot be—such communities under existing social and political conditions, then they are decidedly antidemocratic. This, of course, points to the crisis of conscience experienced by academic humanists who are devoted to the value claims of the life of the mind, to the preciousness of the individual person, and to humane and just socioeconomic arrangements—a crisis aggravated by the fact that technocratic society offers few outlets for intellectual life, especially of the humanist variety, apart from the academy.

The implications of West's work for humanist intellectuals are many, but they spring from one central imperative, that of situating humanities education within political context. This means recognizing the humanities as a cultural battleground, a site of political struggle. Ironically, those who acknowledge this struggle are those who are most likely to be barred from participating in it. Thus, the battle seems to be won by those who deny its existence. Furthermore, the structure and values of the modern university constantly threaten to co-opt even those politically aware individuals who gain access to the field. Such persons, as West argues, often end up "espousing rhetorics of oppositional politics of little seriousness and integrity" while "thriving on a self-serving careerism" (*Evasion* 7). In view of this threat, West maintains that the self-consciously political prophetic humanist must turn for existential sustenance to organizations and associations outside of the academy. He/She must attempt to facilitate "alliances and coalitions across racial, gender, class, and religious lines" for the purpose of contributing to a "culture of creative democracy in which the plight of the wretched of the earth is alleviated" (235).

West, it should be noted, is not at all optimistic about the chances for his project's success. As a member of an elite corps of Ivy League intellectuals (now at Princeton), he is

nonetheless beset by "disenchantment" and "demoralization." His own existential nourishment flows, he acknowledges, from black prophetic Christianity. That tradition
"holds at bay the sheer absurdity of life, without erasing or
eliding the tragedy of life." Without such an enabling tradition, he writes, one risks "actual insanity" (233).

For those who are not sustained by such a tradition, the
state of contemporary culture is even more demoralizing.
This in itself underscores the importance of West's message—the vital need for humanist intellectuals to recover
and transmit traditions of resistance and hope. As Rorty
would be quick to point out, there is still adequate space
within the academy for this activity to take place, even if it
must be done by relatively isolated individuals. And even
though, as West admits, such an endeavor may seem little
more than "an impotent moral gesture," nevertheless he
adds, "in the heat of battle, we have no other choice but to
fight" (8).

West's work in this decade, along with that of others
who share his ethical and political sensibilities, points to a
few practical measures that "disenchanted" academic humanists may take, given the existing structure of the university. Recovering and transmitting traditions of resistance
and hope plus uniting oneself with grass-roots associations
outside of the academy are two of these measures. They are
first steps toward overcoming what Lentricchia refers to as
the particular "moral paralysis" of humanist intellectuals
("The 'Life'" 30).

Education for Creative Democracy:
A Possibility in Today's University?

In the next few pages, I will consider one other practical
measure for use within the existing academic structure, proposed by literary theorist Gerald Graff, as well as discuss the
view, expressed most clearly in an essay by Henry Giroux, et
al. that meaningful prophetic action cannot occur in the
university as it is presently structured.

In a 1988 essay entitled "Teach the Conflicts: An Alternative to Educational Fundamentalism," Gerald Graff develops themes suggested in his book *Professing Literature,* which is a history of the academic humanities in America. In the latter, Graff argues that the conservative notion of a cultural and educational consensus which existed until very recently is a myth. In his more recent essay, he points out that reviving Spencer's question "What knowledge is of most worth?" is certainly a good thing to do, but he argues that this question is not—and seldom has been—one that lends itself to a consensual answer. In fact, based on his research for the above book, Graff maintains that

> [w]hen the university did enjoy a relative consensus on ends and values, this was only because it excluded or subordinated major segments of the population (Jews, non-whites, women, and others). ("Conflicts" 102)

This being the case, Graff advocates a careful distinction between consensus and coherence, or put another way, among various models of consensus. He asks,

> If the ideological conflicts in the humanities are unlikely to eventuate in a common content for education, why not try to make these conflicts themselves the basis for a more coherent study of culture? Why not look at ideological and methodological disagreement as a potential opportunity instead of a paralyzing condition to be cured? (105)

In other words, Graff calls for an approach to the humanities which would "help students to see what is at stake in the professional and cultural conflicts that surround them" (106). This, in turn, requires a "more collective model of teaching and learning," a model aimed at helping students to "correlate and contextualize" whatever material they encounter (107). This model would entail abandoning the search for a contrived ideological consensus, and instead, "teaching the conflicts," as well as their history.

Graff argues further that this more collective approach can take place within existing academic structures. Whether or not he is correct, it seems to me that his ideas are worth considering. Put into action, they would serve the purpose of "making the pedagogical more political and the political more pedagogical," to use the Aronowitz and Giroux phrase (*Education Under Siege* 36). In other words, Graff's approach would raise the political consciousness of students by introducing them to the cultural/political conflicts inherent within the university, particularly the humanities. Thus, in addition to being a thoroughly democratic approach to teaching and learning, Graff's model contains the potential to nurture political participation on the part of students, both in the present and the future.

While faculties made up of political conservatives, liberals, and radicals may never agree on "first principles," there is some indication that Graff's collective model may generate at least a minimal degree of common positive response in that two criticisms of modern humanities education shared across political lines are specialization and fragmentation. It may be, then, that even those who are opposed, for whatever reasons, to Graff's collective (interdisciplinary) model of humanities education developed around the notions of ideological conflict and cultural diversity may still concur on the benefits of an introductory course and a capstone seminar in which such conflicts could be acknowledged, debated, and "contextualized."

Lastly, such an approach, even if implemented only in a minimal way, would foster political self-consciousness and self-criticism among faculty members. It would encourage the ongoing development of one's own philosophy of education and a philosophical dialogue with explicitly political content. This, in itself, would be worthwhile.

Suggestions similar to Graff's have come in this decade from John Trimbur ("To 'Reclaim a Legacy' . . . "), Henry Giroux et al. ("The Need for Cultural Studies"), Michael Ryan ("Deconstruction and Radical Teaching"), Susan Jeffords ("Present Rhetoric and Future Opportunities . . . "), and Stanley Aronowitz ("The New Conservative Discourse"). Furthermore, the venerable culture critic, Raymond Williams, has advocated a "collaborative" approach to "cultural studies" which would nurture "conscious diversity" (in Jeffords 106). Certainly this is a partial list, but one which indicates a passionate "oppositional" concern with the content and character of humanities education in the university.

These thinkers share with Cornel West a progressive and pragmatic orientation. They have abandoned "the quest for certainty," and they recognize the inherently political nature not only of education, but of all culture. Thus, from their perspective, the charges of "relativism" and "politicization" leveled by conservatives are themselves masks for a particular political stance, the rumblings of a once hegemonic culture which has witnessed its own collapse. Moreover, Rorty's liberal pragmatism appears finally as an apology for the status quo, thereby serving a politically conservative function, however much his antifoundationalism irreparably damages hegemonic underpinnings. A major distinction between Rorty and progressive pragmatists is that the latter not only historicize philosophy, they also refuse to depoliticize history, as Rorty ultimately does.

Many of the thinkers listed above advocate structural changes in the academy and so go beyond Graff's suggestion for "teaching the conflicts" within the existing institution. In fact, it is fairly common for progressive pragmatists with prophetic ethical sensibilities to harbor grave doubts as to whether any real change can be effected within the present structure. In other words, such thinkers often suffer Foucaultian moments. Henry Giroux, et al. put it this way:

> Michael Foucault has shown that discipline as a particular strategy of social control and domination began at the end of the classical age and came into dominance in the modern period. Though Foucault is not directly concerned with academic disciplines, much of his analysis applies to these enterprises. . . . To be part of a discipline means to ask certain questions, to use a particular set of terms, and to study a relatively narrow set of things. . . . Foucault's work [helps] us to see how these limitations, this discipline, are enforced by institutions through various rewards and punishments. . . . The ultimate punishment is exclusion

> ... The situation is similarly severe for the new Ph.D. for
> whom the price of admission into the academy is ... co-
> nformity with dominant academic discourses. ("The Need
> for Cultural Studies" 146–47)

Giroux, West, and other prophetic pragmatists seek not only
to encourage interdisciplinary work for the purpose of "con-
certed cultural critique" (although this in itself is a vital
goal) but, in effect, to "de-disciplinize" the academy by

> ... lay[ing] bare the historically specific interests that
> structure ... academic disciplines, the relations among
> them, and the manner in which the form and content of the
> disciplines reproduce and legitimate the dominant cul-
> ture. (156)

The problem, of course, is that "counter-disciplinary"
cultural studies "cannot be housed in universities as they
are presently structured" (155). Hence the need for "counter-
institutions," alliances among "oppositional groups" for the
purpose of "radical social change" (155–56). Giroux et al.
argue further that not only will "disciplinary structures"
remain intact for an unforeseen period of time, but that it
would be "a mistake to locate cultural studies within them."
On the other hand, however, it is important to work for
concessions from the administrators of such structures, as a
matter of tactics. The vital imperative is not to be "resigned
to the role that universities assign us" (156).

Thus Graff's proposal has definite merit even from the
perspective of those prophetic pragmatists who doubt the
possibility of effecting significant change from within existing academic structures. This means that the prophetic
pragmatist must, at least as a stopgap measure, struggle "to
retain enough ... strength to ... do a little justice in the
terms of the great injustice" (Warren 184). Significantly,
there are still traditions of resistance and hope—such as the
prophetic tradition—to nurture such a paradoxical, poignant, and problematic undertaking. Furthermore, these
traditions are much more likely to be recovered and trans-

mitted in the humanities than in any other area of the modern university.

For prophetic pragmatists, who recognize the hegemonic authority exercised by the academy, the logic of domination which characterizes many of the practices carried out in the name of truth and democracy, and who yet continue to work within the institution, the future may well be one of frustration and despair. Yet, many such individuals have adopted Gramsci's maxim (borrowed from Romain Rolland): "Pessimism of the intelligence, optimism of the will" (*Notebooks* 175). In other words, neither moral resignation nor academic escapism is an acceptable option in the long run. The thoroughly human stakes are simply too high.

CHAPTER SIX

Diversity, Equality, and Creative Democracy

Either we will redistribute power so as to provide
for equality of participation and respect and protection or we will perish as a democratic state.

—June Jordan

Society will be moral to the extent that we see it in
constant need of challenge, renewal, reconstruction . . . A moral society will be perpetually
unfinished.

—Robert McAfee Brown

Over one hundred years ago, Herbert Spencer posed his
famous question, "What knowledge is of most worth?" For
many persons educated in the liberal tradition, this question
betrays Philistine sensibilities. Students of the liberal arts
are still taught that the pursuit of knowledge is intrinsically
valuable, that knowledge is good for its own sake, and that
its value—as opposed to its "worth"—lies in the examined
life of the knower. I have been both the recipient and the
bestower of such claims and, in many concrete situations,
they are both appropriate and liberating. But there is a
certain danger associated with them when they are abstracted or decontextualized. For the "knower" is not an
abstract, objective, and disembodied entity. The quest to
know is not disinterested and dispassionate. And in this

very important sense, knowledge is never for its own sake,
but for the interests and purposes of embodied beings who
live out their days in the complex world of experience, history, and politics. Within this context, Spencer's question
takes on its most profound meaning: Whose purposes and
interests, indeed, whose *bodies* are of most worth?

This crude formulation offends the sensibilities of not
only the liberally educated, but of all persons reared to
believe in the moral ideals of democracy, such as equality
and justice. Yet the evidence of history weighs heavily and
offers an unambiguous reply to the reformulated version of
Spencer's query. As June Jordan suggests in a short but
eloquent essay, human diversity has not fared well in a
culture which links power with knowledge, and knowledge
with a particular racial, sexual, and linguistic reality. Jordan points out, for example, that from the moment that
white European immigrants—or invaders—arrived on this
continent, diversity became an "issue," a problem which
needed solving. The solution was a "standard." And the standard was white, European, and male.

Now, however, that standard has eroded. The "privi-
leges of normative identity" no longer belong exclusively to
white males of European descent. This transformation is a
social, anthropological, and historical fact (something empi-
rically verifiable) and commands attention on these grounds
alone. But for those whose allegiance is to the prophetic
tradition and to creative democracy, the transformation is
more than a fact. It is a moral imperative.

Not surprisingly, then, this transformation is at the
heart of recent debates over humanities education, particularly when those debates focus on the need for citizens of a
democracy to think as a "we" in the name of public goods.
Bloom, for example, argues that without transcendent standards and the grooming of those few who comprehend such
standards for positions of leadership, no common public good
can be defined. Rorty counters that "we" can create a common good based exclusively on "our" liberal traditions of
tolerance, free inquiry, and open communication. West responds that the very notion of a "we" is empty and fraudu-

lent without a redistribution of power based on a critical understanding of what constitutes power and powerlessness in capitalist, technocratic society. Thus, as John Trimbur has succinctly observed, "The normative meaning in question here is . . . 'What does it mean to be one of us?'" (113).

As indicated above, there are at least two major understandings of the "crisis" afflicting democracy and liberal education. One is that of Allan Bloom and others of his persuasion. Bloom sees cultural diversity as an issue and seeks to impose a Platonic standard (of "man as man") which will solve the problem of value relativity. On the other hand, Cornel West, drawing primarily on the prophetic tradition, affirms diversity and argues that the real issue is a systematic inequality of socioeconomic power, which is intrinsically related to (but not the exclusive cause of) inequality of political power and participation. From this it follows that for West, the "crisis" of liberal education stems not from cultural diversity, but rather from the fact that the vast majority of modern and postmodern intellectuals fail to acknowledge, let alone challenge, the socioeconomic and intellectual hegemony which precludes equality of political power and participation. Such failure points to the inherent relation between socioeconomic hegemony and the intellectual hegemony manifested in the ethnocentrism and sterile professionalism of academia, which remains captive to the illusion of objectivity.

The character of crisis discourse is multifarious and complex. In one important sense, it serves counter-hegemonic interests. As Sheldon Wolin puts it, crisis rhetoric is "usually followed by a claim that something is deeply wrong in the world that affects us all, and that it will not be solved without active intervention" ("Democracy" 17–18). Wolin's description comes in the context of his critique of Rorty, who, as indicated earlier in this study, is far more concerned with preserving liberal bourgeois society than with intervening to change it. In fact, as Wolin observes, it is difficult to see in what sense a "crisis" could exist at all for Rorty, given his understandings of democracy and philosophy. Rorty not only discredits Bloom's sense of a crisis which stems from cultural diversity and value relativism, but also disregards West's understanding of a crisis rooted in a historically persistent and institutionalized inequality of political power and participation.

One of the realizations which prompted this study became clearer as I proceeded: Although a vast majority of the critical discussion dealing with the condition of liberal education points to the future of democracy as *the* central and motivating concern, little consensus is apparent about what democracy is; about whether or not democratic experience—actual participation in the decision-making processes of those institutions which determine the quality of life in contemporary society—is necessary *for* democracy; about what, if any, "active intervention" is required to open the door for democratic experience; and about what forces and conditions obstruct that essential intervention.

Ironically, the same reports which tout "critical thinking" often fail to attend to one of the fundamental aspects of such activity, the setting forth of working definitions. The most troubling dimension of this omission is the seldom articulated assumption that "education for democracy" is synonymous with education for "helping the U.S. to regain its strategic advantage in the world marketplace," as one uncommonly candid public university president recently put it. The basic presupposition here is not difficult to ascertain: Democracy depends on the political economy of technocratic capitalism *and* North America's domination of that economy. Thus any development which threatens either of these necessary conditions presents at least a potential crisis for democracy, one which requires immediate attention in schools and universities. Here then is another understanding of the crisis afflicting both democracy and education, an understanding which points to the extremely disturbing subsumption of notions of moral and political community under the category of political economy. This understanding, I suspect, is the dominant one in contemporary U.S. culture. Therefore, crisis rhetoric is not by definition counter-hegemonic, but is also a tool employed by those who fear a loss of their own power, security, and prosperity.

Importantly, this understanding of democracy coheres fully with that of neither Bloom or Rorty and stands in radical contrast to that of West. While Bloom at least implicitly accepts the basic assumptions of capitalism, and Rorty makes explicit a similar, but qualified, acceptance, neither of these thinkers subsume democracy under a capitalistic political economy. As Sheldon Wolin points out in a recent essay entitled "Injustice and Collective Memory," subordinating political community to political economy means subsuming democratic citizenship under membership in the dominant economic structure (and membership in technocratic capitalism is always uncertain). West, Rorty, and Bloom are concerned with the moral character of democracy and democratic citizenship in ways which are certainly not restricted to, but have definite implications for, this issue. Here it may be helpful to summarize briefly the contrasting views of democracy and education for democratic citizenship present in the work of the three thinkers central to this survey.

The key to Bloom's understanding of democracy is his claim that "[r]eason cannot accommodate the claims of any kind of power whatever, and democratic society cannot accept any principle of achievement other than merit" (96). Bloom's ideal is thus a meritocracy based on natural law and the liberal notion of equality as fairness of opportunity. If this ideal were actualized, then "those who reason best" would lead, and such leadership is vital because the vast majority of persons are not capable of self-government. Following Plato, Bloom believes that the masses need the guidance of a few "wise men" (philosophers) whose love for the truth and scorn for relativism and historicism make them the "naturally" best leaders and the only individuals fit to exercise moral authority in the public realm.

Education fails democracy insofar as it fails to acknowledge genuine merit and to prepare an intellectual elite for future leadership. Relativism and historicism dominate North American culture, and the dangerous political corollary of these intellectual positions is the tyranny of the majority. The consequence is that moral, social, and political life in the United States is in a condition of chaos and crisis.

For Richard Rorty, democracy is a way of life which requires tolerance, free inquiry, and open communication. It is not objectively superior to other political forms of life, and it needs no philosophical foundations on which to rest. Having come into being largely "by accident," it is the best political system we know, given who and what we are now. Democracy obligates citizens to take responsibility for their own destiny and to slough off notions of an authoritative God as well as the pretensions of Reason.

Democracy is in a precarious condition today because it is caught between those who believe that it cannot withstand the loss of its metaphysical foundations and who acknowledge that loss on one hand, and those who believe that they (and they alone) know the true foundations of democracy and who would impose their own moral and political standards on others, on the other. In either case, the necessary conditions for democracy—tolerance, free inquiry, and open communication—are weakened. Education's task, then, is to help disabuse students of their metaphysical presuppositions and to encourage them to take part in preserving existing liberal institutions, upon which tolerance, free inquiry, and open communication depend.

Cornel West understands democracy as a way of life which requires equality of political power and participation. Such equality is a moral imperative with roots in the tradition of prophetic Christianity (as West has received and now creates this tradition). Keeping faith with this tradition means taking part in the struggle for full and genuine equality and seeking to reveal and counter the forces which work against it.

Democracy is not experienced by a majority of persons in the United States today, primarily because moral and political community has been made subordinate to a technocratic, capitalistic political economy which systematically denies participation to those who are made superfluous by the dictates of that economy. Furthermore, the dominant economic and political culture claims for itself the sanction of a natural order.

This claim is articulated and supported by hegemonic forms of cultural expression which influence and even determine the attitudes and behaviors of persons. A case in point is the historically dominant belief that nonwhite peoples are "naturally" inferior to those of European descent and that it is the task of the latter to bring civilization to the former. Thus, the collective injustice perpetrated against nonwhites has been effectively obscured by vocabularies which turn history into nature. Such vocabularies make cultural diversity, rather than moral and political equality, the central issue.

Education's task is to rid itself of the illusion of objectivity, to envision new forms of solidarity, and to nurture the means of democratic social transformation. This task is obstructed, however, insofar as higher education remains part of an entrenched system of state-corporate institutions which have become increasingly unaccountable to the demos. Thus, those who would work for genuine democracy must look for moral sustenance outside of the academy.

As indicated above, the views of Bloom, Rorty, and West are diverse in a variety of significant ways, but similar in that they are all concerned with the character of moral authority in a democracy, with the meaning of justice and equality. This concern separates all three men from those who subsume the notion of political community under the category of political economy and who thus equate education for democracy with education for assuring the United States's hegemony in the world marketplace. It is fair to argue, however, that the model of democracy and education which has dominated North American history is far more consistent with the normative views of Allan Bloom than with those of either Rorty or West and that this model was developed with the purpose of producing future elites rather than nurturing a democratic citizenry.

Political theorist Sheldon Wolin traces this dominant educational model to the "republican-democratic dualism" which characterizes the original U.S. Constitution. In a highly perceptive essay addressing the "intriguing puzzle" of the popular response to Bloom's book, Wolin observes the following:

> The Founders hoped to combine the principle of rule by a republican elite with the principle of popular consent: real politics for the few, formal participation by the many. Education followed the same pattern. Just as the Constitution made no reference to equality and tacitly legitimated slavery, the inferior condition of women, and unequal suffrage, so it was silent about education. ("Elitism" 48)

Wolin's assessment points to the Platonist assumptions of the Founders, in that "republican-democratic dualism" smacks of the notion of moral authority presented in *The Republic*. As in Plato's utopian political community, education in the United States has been largely understood as a method for separating sheep from goats and for instilling desirable attitudes and behaviors in both groups.

But the prophetic tradition also informs modern notions of moral authority and political community, and Wolin's work—along with that of several others surveyed in this study—is itself a testimony to that influence. As Gerald Graff has consistently argued in the past decade, higher education in the United States has never been as conflict-free as contemporary conservative critics would like to believe. Wolin, too, maintains that a continuing tension has existed between the drive to democratize education and the assumption that education should attend to producing future elites.

While that tension is still very much a reality, a notable shift has occurred in the character of the ruling elites, a shift from an economic and intellectual aristocracy to a corporate technocracy in a society which remains essentially plutocratic. Such a shift, not surprisingly, diminishes the prestige enjoyed by liberal education because of its traditional association with the republican elite. Whereas once the children of well-heeled parents were groomed on the classics for authoritative public positions, today's corporate-state structure requires no acquaintance with humanistic intellectual culture. The new elites are those who effectively serve the interests of an increasingly powerful and privatized political economy.

As Wolin argues, the transformation described above came to a head in education during the Reagan administration. Throughout the 1980s, higher education served private economic interests in an increasingly blatant way, while apologists devised a rhetoric to convince U.S. citizens that a dire situation awaited them all if students were not prepared to compete effectively in the world marketplace. The rhetoric was one of crisis, but neither in Bloom's sense nor in West's.

While Rorty seems largely oblivious to the implications for liberal education and democracy signaled by the above development, both Bloom and West are aware that "something is deeply wrong." But while West understands the transformation itself as a part of the crisis facing all of North Atlantic culture, Bloom's outrage is curiously misdirected. As Wolin observes, rather than focusing his attack on the new technocratic elite, Bloom "relentlessly pursues" the relatively powerless—minorities, women, humanities professors. Does this mean that Bloom intends to provide philosophical justification for an increasingly privatized political economy? While his views may serve such an end in an objective sense, his intentions are, of course, far more difficult to ascertain. What can fairly be said is that he supports fervently the Platonist "republican-democratic dualism" inherent within North American political thought. Furthermore, he wrongly attributes the moral crisis of contemporary society to the democratic tendency toward value relativism, as though, as Wolin puts it, "the demos organized, financed, and advertised what passes for 'mass culture'" (54).

On the other hand, West, who radically challenges the dualistic concept of democracy, presents a rigorous critique of intellectual life in the interest of the corporate state and points to the crisis for democracy heralded by this hegemonic relationship. West and others of his prophetic/pragmatic persuasion point to the monumental obstacles encountered by those who are concerned with education for "strong" and "creative" democracy.

The first of these obstacles is the breakdown of authority of *any* historical tradition in modern culture. This breakdown is directly related to the crisis of the humanities because the assertion that the humanities offer a valuable way of knowing presupposes the authority of historical tradition. To the degree that tradition is not valued, to the degree that it cannot justify itself in an era of technocratic capitalism, the humanities' interpretive approach to moral and political life will be granted little if any authority in the academy or larger society. Working against the humanities' interpretive mode of inquiry are technocratic modes, characterized by instrumental rationality, an insatiable craving for the new, and the authority of experts. These modes represent what Wolin calls "an eternally modernizing mentality," with significant connections to notions of an ever-expanding economy and global hegemony. Thus defending the humanities' way of knowing against technocratic ideology is an intrinsically political undertaking.

A second issue of political significance is the need to discriminate among competing historical traditions and to formulate some means of critiquing their social/moral consequences. Assuming for the sake of argument that technocratic ideology is losing its authority and that a renewed dedication to the value of cultural tradition is about to flower, the postmodern West is still confronted with a history which does not provide a single unified tradition from which to draw. As critics of Rorty have been quick to point out, his attempt to reduce tradition to such a single homogeneous authority simply replaces the "epistemological myth of the given" with an "historical myth of the given." Such a move is thus unacceptable, both philosophically and politically. It not only flies in the face of what anthropologist Clifford Geertz calls the enormous multiplicity of modern consciousness, but also stands in stark contrast to the moral sensibilities of the prophetic tradition, which is characterized by a staunch commitment to the equality and dignity of all persons, especially those who are, for whatever reason, socially degraded. The prophetic drive toward strong and creative democracy thus includes a preferential option for the historically voiceless and powerless.

Those who decry the "politicization" of the humanities are predominantly concerned that the preferential option referred to above obscures the "universal" and "eternal" truths of Western cultural tradition, truths which speak *to* us all but not *through* us all. Claiming the existence of universal and eternal truths is not enough for critics such as Bloom, Bennett, and Cheney; they also pronounce that only certain voices situated in certain places at certain times have articulated those truths. The interpretive mode of inquiry traditionally associated with the humanities is thus denied, for the sensibility nurtured within this mode is one *which understands and treasures the truth of human diversity and ponders the moral implications of that truth.*

When this truth is denied, when diversity is seen as an issue or a problem to be solved, then the need for a certain normative form of moral authority—a form unveiled by the humanities, but not endorsed by the spirit which sustains them—becomes central and in fact takes on greater import than keeping faith with that spirit. When the truth of diversity is embraced, the humanities are understood as a great collection of stories that we humans tell to each other, hoping to make some sense of our lives, hoping to make connections in both space and time, hoping to resist and counter those forces which stifle our humanity, spiritually and physically. Stories are human creations, expressions of the "utopian spirit"; as such, they wield or transmit no absolute moral authority. But to keep faith with a story is to grant it authority and to give it new shape within the context of one's historical moment.

I began this study by pointing to the civil rights movement of the 1960s as an example of historical disputes over the appropriate character of moral authority in a democracy. When Martin Luther King, Jr. elected to take direct action against racial injustice, he was keeping faith with the prophetic story. For the prophet, diversity is not an issue, but equality of participation and respect is. When such equality is denied by those who claim allegiance to a "higher" moral authority, the prophet does not seek to establish superior metaphysical proofs. Rather, he/she *acts* to change the structure of public life so as to nurture equality because without such equality the very notion of moral authority is vacuous at best and oppressive at worst. This ethical orientation is manifested in Jane Addam's observation,

> We have learned to say that the good must be extended to all of society before it can be held secure by any one person or class; but we have not yet learned to add that unless all [persons] and classes contribute to a good, we cannot even be sure that it is worth having. (in Cremin, *Transformation* ix)

Disputes over the appropriate character of moral authority in a democracy are always relevant to the content and character of higher education because education is so relevant to democratic public life. The crucial question for many persons today, however, is whether or not those who would nurture creative democracy can hope to effect any genuine social and cultural transformation within existing academic structures. This question is significantly different from the famous one posed by George Counts in 1932 ("Dare the School Build a New Social Order?"). The challenge in the late twentieth century is not "daring" to create a new social order through education, but confronting the very real possibility that the will to participate in such an endeavor is not enough, given the entrenched character of existing corporate/state-driven educational structures. Yet, the moral sensibility which prompted Counts' question is still alive and well today. And an awareness of this historical moral community is inspiring to those, myself included, who are only beginning teaching careers. I, for one, am tremendously heartened by the example provided by Cornel West (and many others like him, regardless of whether their names appear in this study) of the prophetically faithful, morally engaged teacher and scholar. I have also become increasingly aware of John Dewey's presence just over my shoulder.

Dewey recognized, much more clearly than most, that we are not only parasitic upon tradition, we shape it by acts of interpretation and critique. Taking this task seriously means ridding ourselves of the illusion of objectivity and contributing to a democratic tradition which has not yet become.

Bibliography

Aronowitz, Stanley. "The New Conservative Discourse." *Education and the American Dream.* Ed. Harvey Holtz et al., 203–215. South Hadley, Mass.: Bergin and Garvey Publishers, 1989.

——. *Science as Power.* Minneapolis: University of Minnesota Press, 1988.

Aronowitz, Stanley and Henry Giroux. *Education Under Seige.* South Hadley, Mass.: Bergin and Garvey Publishers, 1983.

Barber, Benjamin. *Strong Democracy: Participatory Politics for a New Age.* Berkeley: University of California Press, 1984.

——. *The Conquest of Politics.* Princeton: Princeton University Press, 1988.

——. "The Philosopher Despot." *Harper's* (January 1988): 61–65.

Bate, Walter Jackson. "The Crisis in English Studies." *Harvard Magazine* (September–October 1982): 46–53.

Becker, Ernest. *The Denial of Death.* New York: Free Press, 1973.

Bennett, William. "The Shattered Humanities." *The Wall Street Journal* 31 Dec. 1982, 10.

——. *To Reclaim a Legacy: Report on Humanities in Education.* The Chronicle of Higher Education 29, no. 13 (28 Nov. 1984), 16–21.

——. "Western Principles Define Standard." *Iowa State University Daily,* 17 June 1988.

Bennett, William, and Terry Eastland. *Counting by Race.* New York: Basic Books, 1979.

173

Berger, Alan. "Academia and the Holocaust." *Judaism: A Quarterly Journal of Jewish Life and Thought* 31, no. 2 (1982): 166–76.

―――. "Holocaust: 'The Pedagogy of Paradox.'" In *Toward the Understanding and Prevention of Genocide.* Ed. Israel W. Charny, 265–77. Boulder and London: Westview Press, 1984.

Bloom, Allan. *The Closing Of The American Mind.* New York: Simon and Schuster, 1987.

Bernstein, Richard. "One Step Forward, Two Steps Backward: Richard Rorty on Liberal Democracy and Philosophy." *Political Theory* 15, no. 4 (November 1987): 538–63.

Bowker Annual of Library and Book Trade Information. 33d ed., ed. Filomena Simora. New York: R. R. Bowker Co., 1988.

Brown, Robert McAfee. *Elie Wiesel: Messenger to All Humanity.* Notre Dame, Ind.: University of Notre Dame Press, 1983.

Camus, Albert. *Les Essais.* Paris: Gallimard, 1954.

―――. *L'Homme révolté.* Paris: Gillimard, 1951.

―――. *Lyrical and Critical.* London: H. Hamilton, 1967.

Canon Busting and Cultural Literacy. National Forum. Phi Kappa Phi 69, no. 3 (Summer 1989): 1–43.

Chang, Irene. "Citibank Changes Credit Card Policy After Discriminated Students Protest." *The National College Newspaper* 2 (September 1988): 14–17.

Chapman, Tracy. "Material World." In *Crossroads.* New York: EMI April Music Inc., 1989.

Cheney, Lynne. "Defending the Humanities." *The Chronical of Higher Education* 33 no. 41 (24 June 1987): 38.

―――. *Humanities in America: Report to the President, the Congress and the American People.* Washington: National Endowment for the Humanities, 1988.

Chomsky, Noam. *Necessary Illusions.* Boston: South End Press, 1989.

Comay, Rebecca. "Interrupting the Conversation. Notes on Rorty." In *Anti-Foundationalism and Practical Reasoning: Conver-*

sations Between Hermeneutics and Analysis. Ed. Evan Simpson. Edmonton: Academic Printing and Publishing, 1987.

Christ, Carol. *Laughter of Aphrodite*. San Francisco: Harper and Row, 1987.

Cremin, Lawrence. *Popular Education and its Discontents*. New York: Harper and Row, 1990.

Cremin, Lawrence. *The Transformation of the School*. New York: Vintage Books, 1964.

Descombes, Vincent. *Modern French Philosophy*. Trans. J. M. Harding and L. Scott-Fox. Cambridge: Cambridge University Press, 1980.

Dewey, John. *Democracy and Education*. New York: Free Press, 1916.

———. *Human Nature and Conduct*. New York: Henry Holt and Co., 1922.

———. "Philosophies of Freedom." In *The Moral Writings of John Dewey*. Ed. James Gouinlock. New York: Hafner Press, 1976.

———. *Philosophy and Civilization*. New York: Minton, Balch and Co., 1931.

———. *Problems of Men*. New York: Philosophical Library, 1946.

———. *The Public and its Problems*. Chicago: Gateway Books, 1946.

Edelman, Mark. Telephone interview with author. 21 July 1989. Iowa State University, Ames, Iowa.

Fraser, Nancy. "Solidarity or Singularity? Richard Rorty Between Romanticism and Technocracy." *Praxis International* 8 (October 1988): 257–72.

Freire, Paulo. "Humanistic Education." In *The Politics of Education*, 111–19. South Hadley, Mass.: Bergin and Garvey Publishers, 1985.

———. *Education for Critical Consciousness*. New York: Seabury Press, 1973.

Geertz, Clifford. *Local Knowledge*. New York: Basic Books, 1983.

————. *The Interpretation of Cultures.* New York: Basic Books, 1973.

Giroux, Henry. *Schooling and the Struggle for Public Life.* Minneapolis: University of Minnesota Press, 1988.

————. *Theory and Resistance in Education: A Pedagogy for the Opposition.* South Hadley, Mass.: Bergin and Garvey Publishers, 1983.

Giroux, Henry et al. "The Need for Cultural Studies." In *Teachers as Intellectuals.* South Hadley, Mass.: Bergin and Garvey, 1988.

Glassman, Ronald. *Democracy and Equality.* New York: Praeger, 1989.

Goodman, Ellen. "Amen to Moral Majority's Retreat." *Des Moines Register,* Iowa, 16 June 1989.

Gould, Stephen Jay. *The Mismeasure Of Man.* New York: W. W. Norton and Co., 1981.

Gouldner, Alvin. *The Dialectic of Ideology and Technology.* New York: Seabury Press, 1976.

Graff, Gerald. Foreword to *Universities and the Myth of Cultural Decline,* By Jerry Herron. Detroit: Wayne State University Press, 1988.

————. *Professing Literature: An Institutional History.* Chicago: University of Chicago Press, 1987.

————. "Teach the Conflicts." In *Literature, Language, and Politics.* Ed. Betty J. Craige. Athens: University of Georgia Press, 1988.

Gramsci, Antonio. *Selections from the Prison Notebooks.* Trans. and ed. Quintin Hoare and Geoffrey Nowell Smith. London: Lawrence and Wishart, 1971.

Greenlee, Sam. "Strategies for Change." ISU Lecture. Parks Library. Iowa State University, Ames, 1974. Audiotape.

Gumbert, Edgar, and Joel Spring. *The Superschool and the Superstate: American Education in the Twentieth Century, 1918–1970.* New York: John Wiley and Sons, 1974.

Habermas, Jürgen. *Knowledge and Human Interests*. Trans. Jeremy Shapiro. Boston: Beacon Press, 1971.

Heller, Scott. "Experts Convened by Endowment Head are Divided in Assessing the Health of the Humanities." *The Chronicle of Higher Education* 34, no. 26 (9 Mar. 1988): 4.

Herron, Jerry. *Universities and the Myth of Cultural Decline*. Detroit: Wayne State University Press, 1988.

Heschel, Abraham. *The Prophets*. New York: Harper and Row, 1962.

Hiley, David. "Edification and the End of Philosophy." In *Philosophy in Question*. Chicago: University of Chicago, 1988.

Hollinger, Robert. "From Weber to Habermas." In *Introductory Readings in the Philosophy of Science*. Ed. Robert Hollinger, E. D. Klemke, and A. David Kline. Buffalo: Prometheus Books, 1988.

———. Introduction to part 5. In *Introductory Readings in the Philosophy of Science*. Ed. Robert Hollinger, E. D. Klemke, and A. David Kline. Buffalo: Prometheus Books, 1988.

———. Introduction to part 6. In *Introductory Readings in the Philosophy of Science*. Ed. Robert Hollinger, E. D. Klemke, and A. David Kline. Buffalo: Prometheus Books, 1988.

———. "The Holocaust, Technology, and Cultural Pluralism." Iowa State University Conference on Religious Ethics and Technological Change, Ames, 28 Apr. 1984.

Hughes, H. Stuart. *The Obstructed Path: French Social Thought in the Years of Desperation 1930–1960*. New York: Harper and Row, 1966.

Hughes, Thomas. "Technology." In *The Holocaust Ideology, Bureaucracy and Genocide*. Ed. Henry Friedlander and Sybil Milton. Millwood, N.Y.: Kraus Publications, 1980.

Hutchins, Robert. "General Education." In *Rethinking Education*. Ed. William F. O'Neill. Dubuque, Iowa: Kendall/Hunt Publishing Co., 1983.

———. *The Conflict in Education*. New York: Harper and Row Publishers, 1953.

Jacoby, Russell. *The Last Intellectuals*. New York: Basic Books, 1987.

Jeffords, Susan. "Present Rhetoric and Future Opportunities in the Humanities." *Liberal Education* 72, no. 2 (Summer 1986): 101–8.

Jordan, June. "Diversity or Death." *The Progressive* (June 1990): 16–17.

King, Martin Luther, Jr. "Letter from Birmingham Jail." In *Why We Can't Wait*. New York: New American Library, 1963.

Koyama, Kosuke. *Mount Fuji and Mount Sinai*. London: SCM Press Ltd., 1984.

Kozol, Jonathan. *The Night is Dark and I Am Far From Home*. Excerpted in *Rethinking Education*. Ed. William F. O'Neill. Dubuque, Iowa: Kendall/Hunt, 1983.

Kren, George, and Leon Rappoport. *The Holocaust and the Crisis of Human Behavior*. New York: Holmes and Meier Publishers, 1980.

Leland, Dorothy. "Rorty on the Moral Concern of Philosophy: A Critique From a Feminist Point of View." *Praxis International* 8 (October 1988): 273–83.

Lentricchia, Frank. *Criticism and Social Change*. Chicago: University of Chicago Press, 1983.

———. "The 'Life' of a Humanist Intellectual." In *The Academic Handbook*. Ed. Leigh Deneef, Craufurd D. Goodwin, and Ellen Stern McCrate. Durham, N.C.: Duke University Press, 1988.

Lifton, Robert Jay. *The Naxi Doctors: Medical Killing and the Psychology of Genocide*. New York: Basic Books, 1986.

———. *The Life of the Self*. New York: Simon and Schuster, 1976.

Lilge, Frederic. *The Abuse of Learning: The Failure of the German University*. New York: Macmillan Co., 1948.

Littell, Franklin. "The Credibility Crisis of the Modern University." In *The Holocaust: Ideology, Bureaucracy and Genocide*. Ed. Henry Friedlander and Sybil Milton, 271–83.

Millwood, N.Y.: Kraus International Publications, 1980.

Lottman, Herbert. *Albert Camus: A Biography.* New York: Doubleday and Co., 1979.

Mansfield, Harvey. "Democracy and the Great Books." *The New Republic* (4 Apr. 1989): 33–37.

McClelland, Charles. *State, Society, and University in Germany, 1700–1914.* Cambridge: Cambridge University Press, 1980.

Melancon, Marcel. *Albert Camus: An Analysis of His Thought.* Trans. Robert Dole. Ottawa, Canada: Tecumseh Press, 1983.

Mooney, Carolyn. "Conservative Scholars Call for a Movement to 'Reclaim' Academy." *The Chronicle of Higher Education* 35, no. 13 (13 Nov. 1988): 1.

National Forum 69, no. 3, Summer 1989.

New Oxford Annotated Bible. Revised Standard Version. New York: Oxford University Press, 1962.

Nussbaum, Martha. Review of Allan Bloom's *The Closing Of The American Mind. The New York Review of Books* 34, no. 17 (5 Nov. 1987): 20–26.

Pierce, Roy. *Contemporary French Political Thought.* London: Oxford University Press, 1966.

Plato. *The Republic.* Trans. Allan Bloom. New York: Basic Books, 1968.

Public Policy Education Project Pamphlet. Ames: Iowa State University Extension, 1989.

Rorty, Richard. "Cartesian Epistemology and Changes in Ontology." In *Contemporary American Philosophy.* Ed. John E. Smith. London: George Allen and Unwin, 1970.

———. *Consequences of Pragmatism.* Minneapolis: University of Minnesota Press, 1982.

———. *Contingency, irony and solidarity.* Cambridge: Cambridge University Press, 1989.

———. "Hermeneutics, General Studies and Teaching." *Synergos Seminars* Ed. Vernon Gras, 2 (1982): 1–16.

————. *Philosophy and the Mirror of Nature.* Princeton: Princeton University Press, 1979.

————. "Solidarity or Objectivity?" *Post-Analytic Philosophy.* Ed. John Rajchman and Cornel West, 3–19. New York: Columbia University Press, 1985.

————. "That Old-Time Philosophy." *The New Republic* (4 Apr. 1988): 28–33.

————. "The Priority of Democracy to Philosophy." In *The Virginia Statute for Religious Freedom: Its Evolution and Consequences in American History.* Ed. Merrill Peterson and R. C. Vaughn. Cambridge: Cambridge University Press, 1988.

————. "Thugs and Theorists." *Political Theory* 15, no. 4 (November 1987): 564–80.

Roth, John, and Richard Rubenstein. *Approaches to Auschwitz: The Holocaust and its Legacy.* Atlanta: John Knox Press, 1987.

Ryan, Michael. "Deconstruction and Radical Teaching." *Yale French Studies* 63–64 (1982–83): 45–58.

Schneidau, Herbert. *Sacred Discontent: The Bible and Western Tradition.* Berkeley: Univesity of California Press, 1976.

Schwartz, Delmore, "The True-Blue American." In *American Literature Survey.* Ed. Seymour Gross and Milton Stern, 683. New York: Viking Press, 1975.

Searle, John. Interview with Bill Moyers. *Bill Moyers' World of Ideas.* Public Broadcasting Service, IPTV, Des Moines, October 1988.

Simon, Paul. "The Boy in the Bubble." In *Graceland.* Burbank, Calif.: Warner Brothers Records, 1986.

Stone, I. F. "Plato's Ideal Bedlam." *Harper's,* January 1981.

Tillich, Paul. "Critique and Justification of Utopia." In *Utopias and Utopian Thought.* Ed. Frank E. Manuel. Boston: Beacon Press, 1967.

Toulmin, Stephen. *Cosmopolis: The Hidden Agenda of Modernity.* New York: Free Press, 1990.

Trimbur, John. "To 'Reclaim a Legacy', Cultural Literacy, and the Discourse of Crisis." *Liberal Education* 72, no. 2 (Summer 1986): 109–19.

Walzer, Michael. *Interpretation and Social Criticism.* Cambridge: University of Massachusetts Press, 1987.

Warehime, Nancy. "A Distinctive Humanism, A Difficult Hope: The Social Ethics of Albert Camus." Master's thesis, Iowa State University, 1986.

Warren, Robert Penn. *All the King's Men.* New York: Harcourt Brace Jovanovich, 1946.

Welch, Sharon. *A Feminist Ethic of Risk.* Minneapolis: Fortress Press, 1990.

———. "An Ethic of Solidarity and Difference." *Postmodernism, Feminism, and Cultural Politics.* Ed. Henry Giroux. Albany: State University of New York Press, 1991.

West, Cornel. Introduction to *Hermeneutics. Union Seminary Quarterly Review* 34, no. 2 (Winter 1979): 67–70.

———. *Prophesy Deliverance.* Philadelphia: Westminster Press, 1982.

———. "Schleiermacher's Hermeneutics and the Myth of the Given." *Union Seminary Quarterly Review* 34, no. 2 (Winter 1979): 71–84.

———. *The American Evasion of Philosophy.* Madison: The University of Wisconsin Press, 1989.

———. "The Crisis in Black Leadership." *Zeta Magazine* 1, no. 2 (February 1988): 22–25.

———. "The Politics of American Neo-Pragmatism." In *Post-Analytic Philosophy.* Ed. John Rajchman and Cornel West, 259–72. New York: Columbia University Press, 1985.

———. "The Prophetic Tradition in Afro-America." in *Prophetic Fragments.* Grand Rapids: William B. Eerdman, 1988.

Winkler, Karen. "A Controversial Philosopher States His Case on Politics, Poetry, and Moral Principle." *The Chronicle of Higher Education* 35, no. 34 (3 May 1989): 7–8.

Wolin, Sheldon S. "Democracy in the Discourse of Post-modernism." *Social Research* 57, no. 1 (Spring 1990): 5–30.

———. "Elitism and the Rage Against Postmodernity." In *The Presence of the Past*. Baltimore: Johns Hopkins University Press, 1989.

———. "Injustice and Collective Memory." In *The Presence of the Past*. Baltimore: Johns Hopkins University Press, 1989.

Name Index

183

Subject Index

Absolutism, xix, 47, 87
Academic humanists, 11, 12, 18,
  110, 120–1, 127, 150–2. *See
  also* Humanistic Intellectuals
Aesthetic norms: classical, 144–5,
  147
Affirmative action, 25–6, 54
Alienation, 81
Anthropology, 146
Anti-intellectualism, 52, 56, 59,
  62
Authority:
  cultural, 19–20, 35–6, 38, 42,
    56, 61–2, 64, 67, 72, 76, 88,
    108, 117, 140, 142, 146–8,
    168
  intellectual, 77, 90
  moral, xviii-xx, xxxiii, xxiv,
    xxvii-xxxii, xxxv, 35, 53–5,
    58, 72, 75, 93, 102–3, 108,
    131, 134, 141, 163, 165–6,
    169–70
  social: 4, 5, 55, 120
Autonomy, 91–2, 98

Buddhism, 43, 45

Capitalism, 15, 57, 62, 103, 113,
  121, 138, 162–3, 168
Censorship, 69

Christianity, xvii-xviii, 43, 45–6,
  48, 91, 134, 136, 138, 152,
  164
Citizenship, xxx, xxxii, 105, 163
Classics, 23, 166. *See also* Great
  Books
Class struggle, 138, 140
Communitarianism, 87
Community, 76, 78, 80, 84, 86,
  112, 115, 117, 122, 124–5,
  128, 162–6
Compassion, xxv-xxvi, 148
Conflict:
  epistemological, 68, 154
  cultural, 153–4
Conscience, 87, 91
Consciousness: oppositional, 150–
  1
Consensus, 74–6, 82–3, 87, 94,
  102, 112, 153
Consumerism, 121
Contingency, 75, 85, 92, 96, 100,
  148
Corporate power, 56, 139
Crisis:
  -of African-American culture,
    149
  -of democracy, xx, xxvii, 31, 68,
    72, 100, 161
  -of humanist intellectuals, 151
  -of humanities, xxxii, xxxiv, 1–
    2, 5, 9, 12, 17, 62, 67, 100,
    106–7, 111